"*Surprises of the Christian Way* was written for people who know little about real Christianity. It is a winsome witness to God's amazing work in the world. Shenk draws from wide experience with other cultures and religions to explain the uniqueness of salvation through Jesus Christ. Some of the non-believing students who studied the manuscript in the early stages have now become pilgrims on the Christian Way. I will share this book with seekers, acquaintances, and friends to introduce them to the healing and hope that God brings into the world. I hope many others do the same."
—*Ervin R. Stutzman, Dean, Eastern Mennonite Seminary*

"For folks who usually see the cup half empty, view the scene with jaded eye, or tend to wring their hands over the current state of things, David Shenk's *Surprises* is a powerful antidote. In many ways, Shenk's book is just a simple reminder—a reminder of the blinding brilliance of the old stories, of rascally characters, and of God's inscrutable ways with his people. *Surprises* convincingly confirms the continuity of the God story today. There can be no better news than that.
—*Lee Snyder, President, Bluffton College*

"The lively experiences of different cultures assist the clear and concise Bible-based call to appreciate the characteristic contribution of Christianity to timeless human questions. Short and respectful representations of other religions and philosophies illustrate the way of Christian faith through traditional and modern theological issues. Questions for personal and group reflection on God, church, redemption by Christ, and responsible daily life are gently tinged with the peaceful and committed Mennonite spirit."
—*Rev. Antanas Saulaitis S.J., Director,*
Lithuanian Jesuit Province

Other Books or Booklets by
David W. Shenk

Mennonite Safari

The Early Church and Africa
(with John P. Kealy)

The Holy Book of God

The People of God

A Muslim and a Christian in Dialogue
(with Badru D. Kateregga)

Justice, Reconciliation, and Peace in Africa

Creating Communities of the Kingdom
(with Ervin R. Stutzman)

God's Call to Mission

Global Gods

Surprises of Grace

Practicing Truth
Confident Witness in our Pluralistic World
(Editor with Linford Stutzman)

SURPRISES
of the
CHRISTIAN WAY

David W. Shenk
Foreword by Myron S. Augsburger

Herald
Press

Scottdale, Pennsylvania
Waterloo, Ontario

Library of Congress Cataloging-in-Publication Data
Shenk, David W., 1937-
    Surprises of the Christian way / David W. Shenk
        p. c.m.
    Includes bibliographical references.
    ISBN 0-8361-9133-1 (alk. paper)
        1. Theology, Doctrinal—Popular works. 2. Christian life—Mennonite
    authors. I. Title.

    BT77 .S525 2000
    230—dc21
                                                                00-058166

The paper used in this publication is recycled and meets the minimum requirements of American National Standard for Information Sciences—Permanence
of Paper for Printed Library Materials, ANSI Z39.48-1984.

All Bible quotations are used by permission, all rights reserved, and except
when otherwise indicated are from the *The Holy Bible, New International
Version*, copyright © 1973, 1978, 1984 International Bible Society, Zondervan Bible Publishers.

SURPRISES OF THE CHRISTIAN WAY
Copyright © 2000 by Herald Press, Waterloo, Ont. N2L 6H7
    Published simultaneously in the United States by Herald Press,
    Scottdale, Pa. 15683. All rights reserved
Library of Congress Catalog Number: 00-058166
International Standard Book Number: 0-8361-9133-1
Printed in the United States of America
Book design by Michael A. King, Pandora Press U.S., in consultation with Jim
Butti, Herald Press; cover design by Jim Butti

10 09 08 07 06 05 04 03 02 01 00   10 9 8 7 6 5 4 3 2 1

To order or request information, please call
1-800-759-4447 (individuals); 1-800-245-7894 (trade)
Website: www.mph.org

Dedicated to
My first granddaughter,
Chloe

My first grandson,
Gabriel

You, my grandchildren,
have reminded me of Jesus,
who surprised everyone by exclaiming,

Let the little children come to me,
and do not hinder them,
for the kingdom of God belongs to such as these.
I tell you the truth,
anyone who will not receive the kingdom of God
like a little child
will never enter it.
—*Luke 18:15-17*

Whoever welcomes
this little child
in my name welcomes me;
and whoever welcomes me
welcomes the one who sent me.
—*Luke 9:48*

CONTENTS

FOREWORD

Sharing the good news of God as a personal God of purpose and grace is one of our greater privileges. This message of grace is a gift to all to whom we present it for it makes faith a possibility. Faith is not a blind wish but a response to evidence. David W. Shenk gives the seeker evidence for faith and shows the believer how to witness amid global pluralism, with respect for diversity as well as with clear communication of our own faith. The Christian community as a minority in the world needs to rediscover the Jesus Way of sharing faith. Presenting the gospel amid other religions is not to be done in an adversarial style but through complementary enrichment of thought, faith, and life.

In *Surprises of the Christian Way*, Shenk thoughtfully and creatively gives us a positive expression of following Jesus that is biblical, concise, and clear. Charitably yet confidently, this text cuts across any particular denominational perspective and presents the gospel as a universal word.

The breadth of the author's illustrations, from literature, science, world religions, films, and mass media all enhance the readability and understanding of the book. His broad experience in the global community, including his youth in East Africa, his own mission service, his travel as a consultant to others in mission, and his current service as dean of the Christian college in Lithuania provide him with unique perspectives to share the inspiration and insights in this text. His pattern of respectful dialogue is compassionate and empathetic as he places the Christian Way alongside other philosophies and religions. His approach is mind-expanding rather than mind-controlling.

A great strength of the book is Shenk's high view of humanness, of the human family each alike created in the image of God. His repeated interpretation of issues from the God-centered aspects of life bring a quality into his presentation that is applicable to the whole of personality, including social and ethical considerations. He consistently sets humanity in relation to our self-giving, suffering God who invites all people into fellowship.

This work is an example of evangelism that makes faith in Christ an option for the thinking person. For the "seeker" in faith Shenk offers insightful guidance in what it means to become an informed Christian as a believer in Jesus. Both respect for one another in the human family and our faith, and response to the gospel of grace calls for openness to the work of the Spirit of God. Evangelism respects the thinking of others; its goal is not to put down another religion but to show what Jesus has to offer that is more satisfying.

In a practical and personable way Shenk combines theology and evangelism, freeing the former from mere arm-chair reflection and the latter from any condecending manipulation. And, in the context of university studies, this text can be a very helpful tool for orienting collegiate minds to the quest for faith in our secular and pluralistic society.

I was a member of the Mennonite Church committee that asked Shenk to provide a "seeker-friendly" book to help pastors and church workers introduce persons to the Jesus Way of faith and life. We are grateful for the careful, creative, and insightful way the author has done this. May the Spirit of God use this work to help many persons come to a satisfying life of faith.

—*Myron S. Augsburger*
  Harrisonburg, Virginia

AUTHOR'S PREFACE

I was surprised when God invited me to join with those who walk life's journey in the Christian way; I was only a child. God extended the invitation to me at night, after I had gone to bed. I could not sleep. There was gentle urgency to the stirring in my soul to say, "Yes," to Jesus Christ. I knew that the Christian way is the journey of those who say yes to Jesus.

I slipped out of bed and knelt in prayer. I thanked God for inviting me to say yes to Jesus, and I confessed my sinfulness. I reveled in his forgiveness. Some minutes later, back in my bed, I still could not sleep, for now I was baptized with joy.

Early the next morning, I slipped out of bed and went to the nearby grass-thatched chapel. It was an African chapel overlooking Lake Victoria, at Mugango in Tanzania, for my parents were among the early Mennonite missionaries to East Africa. I sat alone on the second bench from the rear on the left-hand side by the open window. The bench was backless and made of sun-dried brick.

That morning I had my first beginning-of-the-day conversation with Jesus Christ. I covenanted to follow him all of my life. I knew I had begun the journey of walking in Christ's Way. Many years later I learned that the first Christians called themselves People of the Way.

During my early adolescence, I and others were baptized in a Swahili-language Sunday morning worship gathering in the

11

village of Shirati. The grass-thatched church building filled with a celebration song as 500 voices sang "Ni Siku Kuu!" (Oh Happy Day!)

Several years ago I returned to Mugango. The chapel is no more, for a tornado destroyed it. But the weathered brown clay bench is still there. I stood by that bench with several African friends; with thankfulness, I renewed the covenant with Jesus. The decision to walk life's way in obedience to Jesus is the most decisive and far reaching event of my life.

As a youth, I first read through the Bible, from Genesis to Revelation. I discovered that surprises permeate the Bible. I suppose that is the reason I have continued the practice of reading through the Bible regularly. The surprises of God's extravagant generosity and love as revealed in the Bible give me enduring encouragement.

I have discovered that walking with Jesus Christ is a journey of surprises. The settings in which I have walked in that Way have been most varied: childhood and early teen years in Tanzania, and study at Lancaster Mennonite High School in Pennsylvania, Eastern Mennonite College in Virginia, and New York University in Manhattan.

Grace and I have lived in New York City and Lancaster in the United States, in Mogadiscio and Johar in Somalia, and in Nairobi in Kenya. Responsibilities have included teaching, administration, pastoring, and writing. In our pilgrimage, I have also nurtured the joys and challenges of being husband to Grace and father to Karen, Doris, Jonathan, and Timothy, and recently the gift of being grandfather for Chloe, Gabriel, and Owen.

Living in the Christian Way does not mean everything that happens to me is good. For example, when I unwisely led my family to the Mount Longenaut peak in Kenya's rift valley and a potentially lethal thunderstorm developed above us and around us, that was not good. It was dangerous and terrifying. Yet Christ was present with us in that frightening experience.

Living in the Christian Way is the discovery that Christ is present with me in the good and bad experiences, the joyful and grief-filled events of life. Whether working on a farm in Pennsylvania during my teenage years when my parents were away in Africa, teaching world religions at Kenyatta College in Kenya, or developing the faculty team at the Lithuania Christian College where I now serve as academic dean, the Spirit of Jesus has been and is there, surprising me day by day with his presence in all of life's varied circumstances.

Living in the Christian Way fills me with abiding astonishment. I discover that same astonishment as I meet others who have also said yes to Jesus in societies around the world. The Way is intimate and personal. Yet the Way is also universal. That is one of the wonders of the Christian Way.

My journey has been nurtured by Christians from many traditions: Eastern Orthodox, Catholic, and Protestant. However, my fellowship of accountability is primarily Anabaptist.

Wherever I live I choose to cultivate meaningful membership relations in a particular church. At the present time, I am a member of two congregations: Mountville Mennonite Church in the United States and the Klaipeda Christian Free Church in Lithuania. Students and graduates of the Lithuania Christian College planted the Klaipeda congregation; I would characterize the congregation as having a nontraditional Baptist ethos. My wife and I are members in both; presently we live in Lithuania most of the year, with short residencies in the United States.

This book is informed by my particular church commitments as well as my broader ecumenical experience and involvements. The narrative embraces treasures from my particular church affiliation as well the rich interchurch pilgrimage that has so greatly blessed me.

I am grateful for the generosity of Eastern Mennonite Missions and the Overseas Ministries Department team. In early 1998 they gave a three-month leave of absence for writing. Others carried my administrative responsibilities.

The Lithuania Christian College, where I began serving as academic dean about mid 1998, has also encouraged and freed me to invest significant time in the final development of this book. The rich diversity of this ecumenical liberal arts college has significantly informed and enriched the final version of this manuscript.

The Council of Faith Life and Strategy of the Mennonite Church invited me to write this book. I have appreciated their encouragement and counsel.

The critique of several dozen young adults, both believers and nonbelievers, has complemented the counsel of church leaders and theologians. Feedback from people involved in Millersville University in the United States and students and faculty at Lithuania Christian College has been especially helpful. Sixty third-year students at LCC assessed the manuscript. Most were business majors. Their counsel was quite pertinent.

Several people invested many hours carefully critiquing the manuscript: Dean Pinter, Lorne Dick, Aaron Kauffman, Grayson Paschke, and Martha Yoder Maust. Noteworthy is David M. Witmer, who, as a pastor in a secular university, provided profoundly helpful insights. Linas Andronovas, the General Secretary of the Baptist Union in Lithuania, provided significant insight. The publishing editor, S. David Garber, also provided theological critique. My son Jonathan C. Shenk, a New York City area youth pastor, assessed this effort from the perspective of postmodern urban youth. These creative thinkers have influenced the nature and content of this book. I thank them!

Grace has encouraged me graciously with a cup of tea or coffee and a cookie or two when she felt that a little break just might help the cause along.

—*David W. Shenk*
Lithuania

INTRODUCTION

"Who are Abraham and Sarah?" a neighborhood acquaintance asked us one evening.

My wife, Grace, and I were enjoying refreshment with this bright, young, educated couple in their Mountville, Pennsylvania, home.

"What is the big deal about Adam and Eve?" they continued as they searched for clues concerning a faith their grandparents had likely embraced, but for them had become an irrelevant dimension of their families' bygone heritage.

The vision for this book was planted in my soul that evening. I have written this volume as a response to the questions about the Christian Way that our neighbors and student acquaintances share with us. This book is a commitment to hearing and interacting with the inquisitiveness and perplexities concerning the Christian faith that permeate modern society.

Misunderstandings and ignorance about the Bible and the Christian faith are significant obstacles to any serious consideration of the Christian faith in American culture and other modern and postmodern cultures. In this book I have tried to describe the Christian Way with clarity and relevance in the context of western culture and society.

"What difference does Jesus make?" is the focus question that has guided my writing. This book is an invitation to the modern person to consider Jesus.

The title of this book was formed in my mind in a Muslim mosque in Philadelphia, Pennsylvania on a summer evening in 1997. Muslim friends were hosting about thirty Christian missions trainees for an evening of conversation about faith. The imam (leader of the Muslim congregation) explained the five pillars of belief and the five pillars of duty in Islam. He also assured us that because God is sovereign and all powerful, Jesus the Messiah could not be crucified; he was rescued from the cross unharmed.

The erudite imam concluded, "In summary there are no surprises in Islam, for Islam is the faith of the natural person. Even without revelation, every reasoning person is inclined to embrace the logical truth of Islam."

I asked if I may respond as a Christian to what we had heard. They invited my statement. I confessed, "It might indeed be true that Islam is the religion of the natural person and that there are no surprises in Islam. However, no philosophy or religion of humankind has ever imagined the Gospel. The Gospel is the astonishing surprise that our Creator loves us so totally that he has entered our history in Jesus the Messiah. In Jesus crucified, God is suffering with us and because of us."

Our Muslim friends objected, "It is impossible for Jesus the Messiah to suffer in that way. God cannot love that much. That cannot be!"

The dialogue continued as we encouraged our friends, "Let God be free to surprise us!"

The value of this book was confirmed when I taught a third year college course, Introduction to Theology, at Lithuania Christian College in Klaipeda, Lithuania. LCC is a liberal arts college with an enrollment of about 400 students from a dozen countries; some are committed Christians, others have no Christian commitment. Most have experienced a world view nurtured by the skepticism or atheism of post-communist eastern Europe and the former Soviet Union. The theology course is required for all third-year students regardless of their major. I used a prepublication manuscript of *Surprises of the Christian Way* as a text for the theology course. Students' expressions of appreciation for this text encouraged me.

Our neighbors and societies are often quite skeptical of any surprises, and especially any surprises from God. The Bible is also peppered with accounts of cynicism, indifference, hostility, skepticism, or perplexity; however, the writers of the Bible tried to encourage faith in their world amid the objections to faith that they encountered.

In continuity with biblical faith, I have written in the hope that those who do not know the surprises of the Christian Way might discover and believe the good news of this Way. Readers will discover that the stories link faith to modern life as well as to their personal journeys. The accounts are intended to help the person who has little understanding of the Bible discover the core of the Christian faith.

I also attempted to present the good news to encourage those who are already living in the Way of Christ. I trust that the book will help to equip Christians for faithful living and witnessing in our modern cultures.

Surprises of the Christian Way is intended for three types of readers. The first type consists of casual readers. I hope that many will discover this book to be delightful and challenging personal reading.

The second type consists of study groups. I trust that this book will provide lively study and discussion insights for home Bible study groups, friendly discussion groups, cell churches, Sunday school classes, or university or senior high school discussion and study groups.

The third type consists of college-level introduction to theology classes. This book is intended to be a text for college courses that seek to introduce students to the fundamentals of the Christian faith.

A Study Guide is included at the end of the book. The guide has questions and topics for reflection and discussion for each chapter. The guide suggests background scripture readings for each chapter theme. For study groups who wish to use this book as a Bible study, the Study Guide also includes biblical references for most questions that are presented in the guide.

Recommended readings from the Bible are presented at the beginning of each chapter. The reader will discover that reflecting on those background scriptures before reading the chapter will enrich the understanding of the surprises. I have not included the biblical texts in the manuscript, hoping the reader will hold a Bible in her hands and read the scriptures from the Bible itself. If the reader does not have a Bible, most bookstores will have Bibles available, or you can contact a church in your community and ask how you can obtain a Bible. There are a variety of English versions of the Bible; I recommend the New International Version.

All accounts of events and persons are authentic; however, occasionally I have used a pseudonym.

SURPRISES
of the
CHRISTIAN WAY

1

THE GOD RIDDLE

Background Scripture: Genesis 3:8-10; Exodus 3:1-15
"Is God Dead? In Western Europe, it Sure Can Look That Way," proclaimed the European international edition in the *Newsweek* cover headlines, July 12, 1999.

If regular church attendance (e.g., about 11 percent in Britain and 4 percent in Norway)[1] indicates the relevance God has in people's lives, then the authors of the July 1999 *Newsweek* articles are right. In western Europe more and more people are pushing God into the irrelevant periphery of their lives.

Elaborating further, the feature article by Carla Power observes, "Christianity has become an alternative lifestyle—as wacky as atheism once seemed."[2]

Wacky?

Admittedly some notions about God are wacky. At least wacky from the perspective of the Bible. Here are a few examples of modern notions about God that are very different from God as revealed in the Bible.

God is the old man upstairs.

God hands down weird rules to us that make life difficult and, in fact, quite unhappy.

Faith in God is about pie in the sky by and by, but has nothing to do with bread in my kitchen now.

God is responsible for everything that happens.

God wants to punish bad people.

God is an old-fashioned traditionalist, quite out of step with modern times.

Sometimes people are not really rejecting the God of the Bible; instead they are rejecting false notions about God like these six statements above. On the other hand, I admit that the biblical belief in God is wacky! It is so off the wall that it is really hard to believe what the Bible reveals about God. The Bible reveals that God who created the whole universe, all fifty billion galaxies and more, loves you as much, yes, and even more than a mother loves her infant baby (Isa. 49:15).

That is a surprise so astounding that it really does sound wacky; yet that is precisely the good news that touches Christians with abiding joy. This book is an exploration of that surprise.

If God of the Bible is a good-news surprise, why are churches in western Europe so empty? Why do multitudes of people, not only in Europe, but everywhere, ignore or reject God? Is it because people are rejecting notions about God that are false, like the idea that God gives us rules to make us unhappy? Or are they rejecting the God who loves them? That is the question we will ponder as we consider the God riddle.

Nudging God out of our lives is not unique to modern western Europe. Societies and individuals everywhere are often inclined to do so. In fact, a couple of centuries ago, some of the fathers of the American experiment in democracy seemed rather skittish about God.

For example, the authors of the Declaration of Independence for America based their philosophy of democracy on "self-evident" truths. The Declaration never refers to revealed truth from God. The authors of that declaration seem to have believed that a God who reveals truth is irrelevant to the democracy they were building.

In Euro-North American societies, our neighbors, likewise, are often nervous about God-talk. Many believe that God-talk will encourage truth claims that are destructive to democracy.

Our societies on the whole are convinced that democracy can flourish only when all "values" are equally respected.

Values are splendid, but truth is suspect. Values are fine, because each group has its own kinds of values, but any idea about truth is dangerous. Whose truth will you defend? The truth as taught by Marxism, Islam, or the Church? This concern shows that we realize we cannot consider God without also considering questions of truth.

We are told that people who are committed to God tend to become intolerant in their defense of truth, which is dangerous. Western society calls these people "fundamentalists." They fight for truth, and do such things as burn mosques in India or bomb abortion clinics in the United States. We are told that there is a lot of evidence for how dangerous to democracy dogmatic claims to God's truth are: for example, look at the impasse in Northern Ireland, where Catholics and Protestants have collided violently because of their different understandings of God.

This kind of religious violence is an obstacle to belief in God for many people. Secular Jewish people have told me that it is the different beliefs about God among Muslims and Jews that makes the Middle East peace process extremely difficult. Consequently some people have come to believe that faith in the God of either the Jewish or the Muslim Scriptures is destructive to peacemaking; they believe the only way through the impasse must be a secular humanism.

Other people are dismayed by the mores and practices that religious communities often demand in the name of God or the gods. For example, the caste system in India is anchored in the Hindu religion. The stance of the Catholic church concerning birth control in an age of rapid population growth appalls some people. Many consider the call of the church to sexual chastity to be outdated in an age of sexual permissiveness.

There are, of course, other objections that people face when they consider God. A primary objection I have met teaching college students in post-communist Lithuania is this: if there is a

God, why have we suffered so much? Here is a society where, in a half century, twenty-five percent of the people were either killed or sent to Siberia. Why? Where was God?

What about natural calamities? If God really is involved in history and the one who sustains nature, why did Hurricane Mitch devastate Honduras and other Central American countries with up to seventy inches of rainfall in October 1998? These countries are among the poorest in the world, yet homes, roads, businesses, plantations, and lives were destroyed. Tens of thousands of people made their living on the banana plantations; those plantations were covered with mud or washed away. Many among these people were noteworthy for their faith and energetic involvement in the church. If there is God, why?

These are social or philosophical obstacles to belief in God. However, sometimes we do not fully understand the reasons for belief or nonbelief. The obstacles are personal, perhaps hurtful and painful. A note from a student says, "I am not a believer. Yet when I pray hoping to believe, there is only emptiness. Where is God when I pray?"

Another student confides, "I want to believe, but there are barriers that keep me from belief. At one time I believed in communism. That was a lie. I don't want to be deceived again. Perhaps sometime I will be a believer. For the present, God is the question mark in my life."

These are a few examples of perplexities or objections to faith in God. It is, therefore, not surprising that philosophers, societies, and people everywhere ponder the God riddle. Ten modern approaches to that riddle follow here.

Perplexity about God

1. God is an illusion

That was the conviction of Sigmund Freud, the father of modern psychoanalysis. He believed that the idea of God was the invention of the human mind, because the person and society needed a divine father figure. Freud developed a theory that the belief in one God was a necessary neurosis for societies in transition from a prescientific to a scientific worldview.

Freud believed that holding a civilization together is difficult, because the inclinations of people are very destructive. Belief in God is, therefore, useful in providing the restraints that are necessary for civilization. However, Freud was hopeful that the God illusion would become unnecessary in the future as people embrace the rational truths of science.[3]

2. God is the question

That was the belief of my professor of philosophy at the University of Pennsylvania. The professor placed a small circle in a large circle on the blackboard. The small circle represented what we know. The large circle was a question mark representing what we do not yet know. That question mark is God or religion. My professor then enlarged the smaller inner circle drawing ever wider circles until the inner circle encompassed the outer circle. He explained that as our knowledge grows, God decreases. Eventually knowledge will replace God, for there will be no remaining question mark.

God as the question is sometimes referred to as "God of the gaps." We create God to fill the gaps in our knowledge of the universe.

3. God is everything and anything

That is the belief of the Hindus. Their swamis sometimes gently chide Muslims for believing in only one God or Christians for embracing only a Trinity. Hinduism, we are told, is much more expansive: at least 300 million gods; remember, everything is god, god, god!

The director of nursing of a hospital near our home in the United States commented to my wife, who was hospital chaplain, "People with addictions need a higher power. Each person should choose her own higher power. It might be the metal radiator that heats the room. The higher power is whatever one chooses." This kind of notion that God is everything and anything is called pantheism.

4. God is nature

The New Age movement flirts with the notion that nature is divine, which is similar to Hinduism. The message of the popular 1999 film, *The Thin Red Line*, is that nature veneration or worship takes many forms. This South Pacific war movie views good and evil and all that we are as an expression of nature. One soldier worships the moon; another venerates only himself.

Nature worship might be the personalized divinity in a natural phenomenon that is worshiped, or it might be the phenomenon itself that is venerated. Sometimes nature is understood to be a dead god, as in the Chinese myth of P'an Ku, the first man, a mighty divinity. On his death, his decaying body became the natural features of China.

Nature gods might appear to be benevolent. In reality, however, these gods, whether dead or alive, are quite dangerous. A clan might worship the harmless butterfly, but once nature worship is embraced, it seems there are no boundaries where that path might lead. For Israel in the Old Testament, that apparently harmless direction away from God the creator to the worship of nature eventually led the Isrealites to offer their own children as sacrifices to the gods of nature (Molech).

An African friend once told me, "We used to worship nature and especially the leopard. Our leopard god was terrifying."

5. God is irrelevant

That was the teaching of Gautama Buddha. The Buddha was an agnostic, uncertain whether there is a God or gods. But he was convinced that no divinity can provide personal peace or nirvana. The person needed to acquire his own salvation and peace, and any notions of help from God were misguided.

In modern times God is just as irrelevant for many people as Buddha thought him to be. For example, many modern people trust in scientific medicine when they are ill. They never ask God for healing, or thank God for the healing that medicine and the body's healing powers might provide. God is alright for weak people, but irrelevant for strong and intelligent folk.

A century ago, most Europeans traveling in tropical Africa eventually died of malaria. Hundreds of missionaries, explorers, and traders died. In the summer of 1999, my wife and I also traveled into tropical Africa. We bought anti-malaria medicine at the drug store in Pennsylvania before we left, and we survived the malaria-carrying mosquito bites. We survived, not because we prayed more fervently than the missionaries a century ago, but because of the modern gift of anti-malaria medicines.

It is not surprising that many people view science as their savior. Why trust in God to achieve our goals? After all, people might comment, it was applied science, not prayer, that placed Neil Armstrong on the moon.

6. God has gone away

This is the philosophy of African traditional religions. These societies have several thousand myths describing the departure of God.

For example, the Akan of Ghana tell of a woman pounding grain with her mortar and pestle. God was very near, so she hit him in the face with her pestle. In anger, God went into the sky. She was terrified by what she had done, so she and the children collected all the mortars in the village and built a tower of these little wooden barrels.

The woman climbed to the top of the tower to take God's hand to invite him to return to her village. She was almost in reach of his hand and called to the children to find one more mortar to make the tower high enough. The children found one more, but alas it was a mortar at the bottom of the tower. As they grabbed it, the whole tower collapsed and the woman fell to the earth on top of the jumble of mortars. The meaning of the myth is obvious to the Akan people: no tower will ever be high enough to reach God. God has gone away and will never return.

Of course, not just in African societies do people believe God has gone away. The philosophy of deism has taken deep root in Western culture where the notion prevails that God created the world and humanity, but then left us on our own. The Akan myth and the philosophy of deism agree. God has gone away.

7. God is evolutionary

As noted above, Sigmund Freud believed that the "illusion" of one God (monotheism) evolved because of the need for structure and control that civilization requires. A contemporary of Freud, the pioneer anthropologist Sir James George Frazer, also defended the notion that religions evolve. His classic, *The Golden Bough* (1922), laid the foundations in anthropology for the theory that belief in personalized gods or God has evolved from original universal beliefs in magic.

Today the assumption that notions about God are the consequence of social evolution permeates Euro-American culture. How did people come to believe in God? Freud assumed evolution. So do other disciplines. Like Frazer, many anthropologists assume that monotheism evolved from early beliefs in magic and nature divinities. An assumption embraced by many sociologists is that God is the result of the evolution of the belief systems of societies that are moving from tribal identities to more universal social relationships.

God is not really objectively there; rather, God is only in our minds, a result of the evolution of culture and society.

8. God is myth

Myth, as I use it, carries two meanings, as described below.

First, myths are stories that interpret our human situation. The story embodies our understanding of truth. For example, the story of the Akan women and the tower of mortars described above is a myth. The value of the story is not based on whether the narrative is objective history. Even though it might be that no Akan woman has ever built a tower of mortars to reach God, the meaning of the story is nevertheless profound. Historical data is irrelevant to the understanding of truth embodied in the story. The meaning of the story (myth) is that God has gone away and will never return.

Euro-North American societies are awash with the notion that God is also mythical. There is no objective truth or God behind the belief in God. This is not to say that the belief in God has no value. Myths have value because they communicate a people's understanding of meaning and truth. Although people might believe that the notion of God is myth, they might also insist that there is value in the myth. That was Freud's stance.

Second, myth also refers to the fusion of divinity with nature. For example in many pre-Christian religions in the northern hemisphere, when the god died, winter came. When the god resurrected, spring was at hand. The activities of the gods and the cycles of nature were the same. Myth in this sense is akin to nature worship.

9. God is the first cause

The advances of science increasingly reveal the complexity and organizational sophistication of nature. How can such design develop? Multitudes assume that there must be a Creator who is the first cause.

This is not to say the Creator is present or concerned for us. The Creator is like a clock maker who built a clock but has no further involvement in its workings. This is to say that God has put the universe and earth together but is not involved now. As mentioned in Number 6 above, this notion is known as deism.

10. God is a universal principle

There is nothing personal about God. Rather, God is a principle, such as wisdom or the ideal good. Plato, the fifth-century B.C. Greek philosopher, taught that the ideal good is a universal principle that we can perceive through intuition.

Such philosophical notions are pervasive in Euro-North American culture. These ideas provided a philosophical framework for the development of Marxism. In Marxism the universal principle is dialectical (reasoned and logical philosophy) materialism. Marxism teaches that we discover the universal principle through the tools of philosophical analysis, not through revelation.

The God Who Speaks and Acts!

The Bible reveals a radically other God than these ten varied approaches to the God riddle. The God of the Bible is an astonishing surprise, for he is the righteous personal God who loves us and encounters us. He is the God who reveals himself to us through his acts and his speech. God meets us in our story; he is the God of history. It is this reality that makes the Bible such an astoundingly different book than any other.

Bible history is surprising

The Bible is an unfolding five-part historical drama. It is the drama of God working in human history. The first three parts of the drama are included in the Old Testament, and the last two parts are the New Testament story; the Bible consists of both the Old Testament and the New Testament.

The first drama is a remarkable account of universal history (Gen. 1-11). This history provides a foundation for understanding the reality of creation, human existence, and the development of nations.

This universal history declares that all people come from the same parents, Adam and Eve, and are created in God's image. Such convictions are the foundations for healthy nationhood and relations between nations. The first part of the Bible is a remarkable insight into universal international history.

The second drama is the account of God calling a people to be his chosen nation among the nations, so that they will be a light to humankind. This people is Israel. Israel's story begins with God's call to Abraham in Genesis 12; God promised Abraham that through his seed all nations will be blessed.

The story unfolds as an account of Israel, the descendants of Abraham and Sarah, becoming a nation among the nations. The story continues through the portions of the Old Testament that were written before Israel was taken captive by hostile nations between the eighth and sixth centuries B.C.

The third drama is Israel's experience during and after its captivity. In these portions of the Old Testament, Israelites are gaining new understandings of what it means to be the people of God. The people also yearn for the coming of the Messiah who will extend God's kingdom to the ends of the earth.

The fourth drama begins with the New Testament. The gospels that are the first four books of the New Testament announce that Jesus is the Messiah and describe his life, teaching, and ministry.

The fifth drama is the New Testament account of the formation of the church and theology and mission of the church. The church is the people who believe that Jesus is the Messiah. The New Testament describes the church as a universal community of faith from nations around the world. This is understood as a fulfillment of God's promise that through Abraham all nations will be blessed.[4]

These five dramas are the work of God. He speaks and acts in the human story.

God Does Not Speak to Me!

"But God does not speak to me," a college student lamented. "What does it mean for God to speak?"

We will explore that question. The Bible itself is an exploration of that question. The biblical writers contributed their understandings of God acting and speaking. It is likely that at least sixty people contributed their written observations to the Bible; these writers span a period of a thousand years. They were learners, discovering who God is and discerning how to hear God. It is wise to explore what they have written.

Tuning in to the Right Channel

Hearing God speak and seeing God act might be compared to radio and television. For forty years I have listened to British Broadcasting Corporation (BBC) news about once a day. To hear that news, I must tune in to the right channel. If my channel is wrong, I will not hear the BBC. Likewise if I want to see BBC news, I must tune my television to the correct channel for receiving BBC.

For a thousand years, biblical writers were tuning in to God and they share with us what they have heard God say. Equally important, they reveal for us the right channel so we might also hear God and speak with God. For example, James, who wrote a letter for the early church, observes, "Do not merely listen to the word, and so deceive yourselves. Do what it says" (James 1:22).

Listening to God but not obeying God is an example of being tuned in to the wrong channel. The Bible guides us by revealing the acts and speech of God and showing us how to tune in so that we also can hear and see God at work.

Realize, it takes no radio specialist to tune into BBC news. Likewise, tuning into God does not require special techniques or theological expertise. In fact, Jesus commended little children for their readiness to hear. It is this quality of being tuned in to hearing God that makes the Bible such a special book, and this exploration of the Christian Way will interact closely with the Bible.

Later in Chapter 12, I will describe more fully the nature and composition of the Bible.

The God who Meets us

My New York University professor of world religions was right when he used to exclaim in his lectures, "The most significant difference between faith in the Bible and all other religions is this: In the Bible the righteous personal Creator God encounters people, calling on them to repent!"

The Bible provides no philosophical or theological proofs for God. It simply announces, "In the beginning, God. . . ." The first paragraphs of the Bible move right on from that simple announcement to describe God speaking, working, and creating, then meeting and confronting the first human couple.

The God of the Bible not only reveals himself; he also seeks us, meets us, and encounters us. The tools of philosophy cannot reveal God to us; only God can reveal himself to us and seek us. It is for this reason that the Bible is not a philosophical treatise.

The Bible is primarily a history book; it is also a book of poetry, wisdom, counsel, and admonition. But the biblical writers avoided philosophical speculation. Rather they sought to describe and reflect on the acts of God as he seeks us and meets us. That awareness and reflection on the acts of God is the astonishing character of biblical history. What, then, are these surprising acts of God?

First, God has acted as the creator of the universe. In the Bible's first chapter we read that "God said, 'Let there be. . . .'" In poetic beauty, the Bible pictures God speaking seven creation commands to form the earth. Each command brought forth an aspect of the good earth and life as we experience it (Gen. 1).

Second, God speaks and acts in history (Gen. 1, 2). This is why the Bible is fundamentally a history book; it is an account of God's revelation acts in history and our response to him. As mentioned above, these acts of God in the biblical narratives are a five-act drama: the nations, the formation of Israel, Israel's experience of exile, Jesus as the Messiah, and the formation and mission of the church.

The next chapters will describe more of the speech and acts of God in our human experience. However, for the present I emphasize this core dimension of biblical faith: through his acts, God reveals himself as our loving, righteous, personal Creator, who seeks us, meets us, and calls us.

This means that the Creator God of biblical faith is quite other indeed from the ten views of divinity described at the beginning of this chapter. The otherness of God as revealed in the Bible will become more evident as we explore the biblical narrative in the chapters that follow. First, however, I offer a brief summary.

Our Creator Confronts the God Riddle

1. Our Creator is not an illusion; God is real (Gen. 12:1). Any God illusion created by a civilization reinforces that culture. We invent illusions; they never talk back to us or confront us. However, the biblical God confronts all people and cultures calling for the changes righteousness requires.

2. Our Creator is not the question; God is the Creator of the whole universe (Gen. 1:1). He is creator of both what we do understand and what we do not understand; he is the designer of both the realms of our questions and our answers.

Just because I might understand how the transmission of my car works does not mean that I should conclude that no engineer designed that transmission or that I need no counsel from the manufacturer on how to care for it. Likewise, our Creator is worthy of respect both in the realms of human knowledge and in those arenas of creation we do not yet understand.

3. Our Creator is not everything and anything; God is the One who is "other" (Heb. 11:3). Biblical faith calls us to worship the Creator and not the things or creatures he has created. Likewise we are called to turn away from the gods people create. Only our Creator is God.

4. Our Creator is not nature; God created all nature (Rom. 1:18-25). The worship of nature is therefore misdirected and ensnares people in the cycles, fatalism, and even violence.

5. Our Creator is not irrelevant; God is totally relevant (Exod. 3:1-12). God is real and relevant to the real world we live in. God might be irrelevant to our wrong and selfish goals, but our Creator is totally present and concerned for our well being.

Because of scientific advances, some do consider God to be irrelevant. That is not wise or right. As mentioned above, I acknowledge with appreciation that anti-malaria medicine helped to preserve my health during my safari to East Africa. However, it is God who has given us the ability to understand malaria and its cure. He deserves our gratitude, not our disrespect for the advances of science.

6. *Our Creator has not gone away; God seeks us* (Gen. 3:8-11). We have turned away from God but God has not turned away from us. God is present; he has not gone away. Yet where is God when a person seeks God and feels only silence? We will explore that question in later chapters.

7. *Our Creator is not evolutionary; God reveals himself* (Exod. 3:13-15). God in the Bible is radically different than all other ancient Middle Eastern or even global understandings of divinity. For example, the opening phrase of the Bible was a tremendous confrontation with all other world views throughout the ancient Middle East, "In the beginning God created the heavens and the earth" (Gen. 1:1).

All the other religions worshiped nature gods. There was no notion in the surrounding societies of God who is other than nature creating the heavens and the earth; yet here that truth appears recorded by the biblical writers.

The biblical break with other Middle Eastern worldviews is so radical that it cannot be satisfactorily explained as the evolution of notions about a creator. W. F. Albright, a leading archaeologist of the twentieth century, states that it is an "impossibility"[5] that biblical monotheism is the consequence of religious or social evolution. He observes that the biblical break with other religions is too radical for that kind of explanation.

Of course, God reveals himself progressively; we don't learn all there is to know about God in Genesis, the first book of the Bible. However, revelation, not religious evolution, is the only satisfactory explanation for the difference of the biblical God from all other understandings of divinity.

8. Our Creator is not myth; God reveals himself in events (Psalms 105). The core of biblical faith is historical event, not myth, either in the sense of a truth-revealing story or a divinity/nature myth. The Jewish theologian, Emil Fackenheim, describes these respective events in history as "root experience" that provides an "abiding astonishment."[6]

9. Our Creator is not just the first cause; God creates and sustains the universe (Col. 1:16-17). He is personally, actively, and presently engaged.

10. Our Creator is not a universal principle; God is personal (Exod. 3:14). The Creator is not the impersonal ideal good or universal principle of the philosophers. God is righteous, personal, and relational. The God of the Bible is the covenant God inviting people into joyous fellowship with him and with one another.

Philosophers as diverse as Plato, fifth-century B.C. Greek, or Kant, nineteenth-century German, never taught a personal righteous God. Tragically, neither did Karl Marx.

The philosophers reflect on great ideas; sometimes the ideas are quite helpful, and other times diabolical. A central idea of Marx's philosophy was dialectical materialism; for Plato, it was the ideal good. Although philosophers debate about such ideas, they are quite other indeed than the God of biblical faith who is personal and real.

You are not an idea; you are a real person. The same is true of God. Philosophical ideas can never encompass God and they are not the same as knowing God. There is only one way to know God, that is to meet God. To meet God is indeed an astonishing surprise; that surprise is what we will explore in this book.

• • •

We have explored the riddle of God. We have observed that many people consider God to be a problem and they are convinced that committed belief in God can be quite dangerous.

Others are perplexed about the issues of suffering, injustice, or the wrongs and violence that people do in the name of God. Still others are searching for God, but they have not yet found the God they are looking for.

Our exploration of the riddle has included ten modern approaches to the God question. Surprisingly we found that in the Bible, God himself enters into our conversation concerning the God riddle by revealing himself to us through his speech and action.

Our Creator reveals himself as quite other indeed from the modern approaches to God we have considered. None of these ten orientations suggests or imagines that God loves us; yet that is the core reality of biblical revelation. Later chapters will explore reasons for the belief that our Creator loves us.

A study guide for each chapter is included at the end of the book. The guide consists of focus questions and suggested biblical readings for further study and reflection.

2

THE GOOD EARTH

Background Scripture: Genesis 1

My college astronomy course was delightful. We chuckled with amazement when our professor told us there were three billion stars in the Milky Way Galaxy and probably 3,000 other galaxies in space. That was four decades ago.

The Hubble telescope now orbiting 370 miles above the earth is revealing a universe of power, grandeur, enormity, and age that is even more unimaginable. There are 300 billion stars in the Milky Way. As for other galaxies, astronomers estimate thirty to fifty billion of them.

Astronomers have been using Hubble to look to the outer edges of the universe. This exploration is known as operation deep field. Hubble's operation deep field tells us that the universe is thirteen to fourteen billion years old, and that there was a time about eleven billion years ago when the lights (stars) throughout the universe went on "as if every chandelier in a mansion were flicked on simultaneously on a moonless night."[1] Of course, every year new stars are formed, but there was a time several billion years ago when a dark universe was suddenly alight as hundreds of billions of stars began to glow all at once.

It is not only the grandeur of the universe that astonishes us, however; we are also amazed as we explore tiny cells or atoms. For example, in 1998 biologists for the first time unraveled the genetic composition of an animal, a microscopic roundworm known as *Caenorhabditis elegans*. The study of this worm's genome was an intense ten-year project. The DNA of this minute worm consists of ninety-seven million chemical components. It contains 19,099 genes. The written formula for this worm's DNA, if printed in a newspaper, would take 2,748 pages![2]

Bruce Roberts, president of the National Academy of Sciences, commented, "We always underestimate the complexity of life, even of the simplest processes. So this is only the beginning of unraveling the mystery of life."[3]

God Created!

Earth has a front seat view of the universe. We humans are in that front seat where we can explore the wonders of the universe and creation. We are capable of discovering some dimensions of the mind of the Master Designer, who is God the Creator. The Designer is a sophisticated mathematician; the universe reveals intricate plans and mathematical precision amid apparent randomness.

Why should beings exist on Earth who are formed of the stuff of the universe, but who are also capable of exploring and deciphering the intricate complexity and design of the universe? Why should the patterns of the earth, the solar system, and the universe delicately converge in a manner that makes human life on earth possible? Even the slightest deviation in any of millions of different patterns would make human life an impossibility.[4]

Astronomers speak of that moment when the lights in the universe began to go on as the Big Bang. Cosmologist Stephen Hawking points out, "If the rate of expansion one second after the Big Bang had been smaller by even one part in a hundred thousand million million, it would have recollapsed before it reached its present size."[5] That kind of precision demands sophisticated planning and engineering genius.

A wristwatch has never been formed by shaking metal in a container a billion times. Neither do explosions create wrist watches; the heat in the furnace that extracts the metal from the ore that is used to form the wrist watch is the controlled and planned use of potentially destructive heat. Rational beings make watches.

A Master Designer must also have formed the universe. However, the issues of belief or nonbelief in the Creator are much deeper than questions of evidence. A conversation with my friend, Jim, illustrates the point. He and I were both developing our doctoral dissertations in a similar area of study. Jim was a professed atheist.

Driving together on an expressway I asked Jim, "When will you become a believer?"

"Never!" he replied. "You see, the theory of evolution has displaced the God hypothesis."

"Please make a fist, then open your hand," I entreated him.

Quizzically, he obeyed.

Then I asked, "Do you really believe that this amazing phenomenon we have just observed is the result of the evolution of chemicals? Are you entirely convinced that no Master Designer has been involved? Your ears heard my instructions, your mind then informed your hand. Through an intricate system of electrical impulses traveling through your nerves, the tendons in your hand responded to the command to make a fist and then relax your hand. What has happened in these seconds is astounding.

"However, you state that no Rational Intelligence has designed the capability of speech, sound waves, ears, brain, nerves and electrical impulses, tendons, and hands that have been involved in what has just happened between us."

Jim responded, "No, there has to be a Creator. But I still resist believing, because if I believe, I will need to be reconciled to my father, from whom I'm estranged, and that I will never do."

I probed, "So the issue of belief or nonbelief has nothing to do with evolutionary theory. It is a moral issue. It has to do with the implications of personal commitment to our Creator, not evidence."

"That's right," Jim replied.

"In your university classroom, however, you teach that the theory of natural evolution is a more satisfactory explanation of the mystery of life on earth than belief in a Creator. You say that even though you know that you are telling a damned lie."

"Yes," Jim commented with wry candor. "Most of us professors do the same. We call that lie academic sophistication."

The conversation with Jim revealed that for the two of us, our radically different beliefs of the meaning and nature of the earth was anchored in our beliefs about God; Jim did not believe in God and I did believe.

What Is the Earth?

Our belief about God determines our understanding of the nature of the earth. The ancient Babylonians believed the earth was the body of the dead god, Tiamat, and was quite dangerous. Hindu friends have told me that the earth is a tragic accident. In contrast to such notions, the biblical view of the earth is based on the belief that God created the whole universe including the good earth.

We will explore briefly four beliefs about the earth that are different than the biblical Scripture.

1. *The earth has oneness with divinity.* I shall use the term *ontocratic* to describe the belief that nature and divinity have oneness. The Dutch historian, Arend Theodoor van Leeuwen, has introduced this term as a helpful understanding of belief systems that do not believe God is other than creation.[6] The ontocratic worldview permeates religions not transformed by biblical revelation.

At one time in Egypt's ancient religious development, the sun (Aton) was proclaimed the one true god by the Pharaoh Ikhnaton. However, this development was not in any sense biblical monotheism, nor was it an evolutionary step toward biblical monotheism. Aton worship was monotheistic nature worship. Three or four thousand years ago, in Egypt as well as all other ancient societies, people worshiped nature gods; biblical faith is the one exception.

The worship of nature might appear to be harmless. However, terror lurks in the gods of nature. Visit the temples dedicated to the gods of nature anywhere. Most often the legends depicting the gods of nature are descriptions of torture and death. The gods of nature are capricious, often immoral, and quite often frightfully dangerous.

2. *The earth is illusion.* Both Hinduism and Buddhism view the earth as a fundamental irrelevancy. Salvation is escape from the material world. These faiths view the material world as a distraction from salvation. In Western societies Christian Science embraces similar illusion themes as those that nurture Hindu and Buddhist attitudes toward the material earth.

3. *The earth is less good than spirit.* This was the conviction of Plato and the Greek philosophies that derive from his teachings. The realm of ideas was the good, not the earthly and material world.

4. *The earth and material universe are the only reality.* This is the philosophical foundation of all modern materialistic philosophies; these philosophies teach that the physical world is the only reality. Marxism with its ideology of dialectical materialism has been a classic example of materialism.

Marxism taught that the value of the person is the work he produces. At death the person is like a stone. There is nothing beyond death except the absorption of the body into the earth.

It should not surprise us that materialistic philosophies often exploit the earth, not care for it. In the communist societies of the former Soviet Union, the legacy was one of devastating destruction to the environment. These social systems sought to wrench material wealth from the earth regardless of the cost to its well-being. There was no sense of accountability to be good stewards of the earth.

We have reviewed four alternatives to the biblical affirmations concerning the earth. None of these four very different understandings of the earth affirm that the earth is good. None of these views remind people that they are accountable to develop and care for our planet.

A Good Creation

In contrast to these four alternatives, the biblical proclamation is dramatic and surprising.

"In the beginning God created the heavens and the earth" (Gen. 1:1).

"God saw all that he had made and it was very good" (Gen. 1:31).

God created the heavens and the earth in a six-day orderly sequence. (Note that most biblical scholars view these passages as poetry communicating the wonder that God is the creator of the good earth!) The first chapter of Genesis describes the unfolding panorama of creation.

First, light and then day and night were created (3-4).

Second, the atmosphere was separated from the waters (6-8).

Third, continents, islands, seas, and vegetation were made (9-13).

Fourth, the rhythm of the seasons was governed by the sun, moon, and stars (14-19).

Fifth, sea creatures and birds were created (20-23).

Sixth, land creatures, mammals, and people were made (24-27).

Seventh, rest!

As the drama of creation unfolded, God looked on his handiwork with joy and satisfaction. Six times he exclaimed, "It was good" (4,10,12,18,21,25). However, after he created mankind, God exclaimed, "It was very good" (31).

A good earth is not a perfect earth. However, God's expectation is that people will work with God to develop the good earth into a better earth. Without people, the earth is only good. With human beings at work cooperating with God in developing the good earth, the earth has the potential to become very good.

Science and Development

These biblical creation themes have provided a worldview that has nurtured scientific inquiry and the technological revolution. It is not an accident that the global revolution in technology began in western Europe in the context of a thousand years of immersion in biblical faith. It was a Christianized society that provided the worldview necessary for science and technology to first flourish as enterprises devoted to human well being.

We recognize that the church authorities sometimes opposed the discoveries of science. High school students learn of Galileo's collision with the church when his telescope helped him discover that the earth revolved around the sun (1564-1642). Science stretched the church's sensibilities; yet all of the early European leaders of the scientific revolution viewed their research as an authentic expression of their Christian faith.

Galileo's experience provides helpful insight for the need for science to respect faith and for the church to hear the discoveries and insights of science. The church needs science, but science also benefits from the insights of Christian faith. Without a commitment to accountability to the Creator, science can become a destructive idolatry. Without science the church can be captivated by superstitions.

The contemporary theologian, Walter Wink, comments,

> A central element in Christianity's appeal over against senescent paganism was precisely its capacity to break the spell of nature and its gods, to distance itself from the onslaught of sense impressions and to establish a new

and independent relationship with the physical universe. This liberation was heady, but was guided by . . . religious piety and ethics. . . . [7]

The notion that people should care for and develop the earth for human well-being and the good of the earth is largely absent in cultures until they are exposed to the "salt" of biblical faith. The same is true of the use of scientific technology in the development enterprise. That might surprise us.

Today development is a goal of most societies. Our news media write about the aspirations of the developing world. Some societies such as Japan have very small Christian communities and yet they have become highly technological and development oriented. That is true; yet the origins of the scientific revolution with a commitment to using scientific discoveries to improve human well-being were first nurtured in societies whose worldview had been transformed by the presence of the church. Even in Japan the scientific/technological revolution commenced after the "salt" of biblical faith had begun to inform the culture through the presence of the church, small though it was. Biblical faith is distinctive in nurturing such commitments.

Let me share a personal story. In June 1999, my wife, my sister, and I visited remote (a six hour walk to the nearest bus stop) Kisaka in Tanzania where my parents had served as pioneer missionaries.

During the evening meal the elders of the community commented, "Your parents saved our community from death."

"What do you mean?" we asked.

"Before the church became present in our community, eighty percent of the babies died of malaria. We thought they died because the grandparents had bewitched the babies. So we killed many of the grandparents.

"When the church became present it brought medicines based on scientific research. The babies stopped dying. At the same time the Gospel taught us to turn away from witchcraft and the nature gods that empower witches. (One of the pastors told me that his grandmother had uncanny powers through her worship of the hyena.)

"Our children lived, and we stopped killing the grandparents. Our tribe is now growing, thanks to the gospel and the church your parents brought to our community!"

Biblical Themes and Development

What are the biblical themes that have nurtured the kind of scientific and technological revolution that has touched even remote communities such as Kisaka in the form of modern medicines? What is it in biblical faith that encourages a commitment to development? Why did my parents as Christian missionaries feel that it was so important to introduce science and technology (a microscope) into the Kisaka community? We note five biblical themes that address such commitments.

God is other than the earth

Imagine plowing a field if you believed that the earth is a god. That is what the Kekchi of Guatemala have believed for centuries. So before plowing, they need to offer sacrifices to the earth god asking permission to scratch the back of god.

In that worldview, there is no theological need to care for or develop the earth. One does not need to care for gods or develop them; one placates and pampers the gods. A farmer can offer sacrifices to the gods of earth, and then contribute to erosion with his plowing. What happens to the earth as a result of his plowing is not his responsibility; that is the responsibility of the divine earth. His primary responsibility to the earth is to offer sacrifices and prayers, not care for and develop the earth.

Obviously there are many variations of the notion that the earth is divinity. I do not mean that wherever people believe the earth is divine there is no agricultural development, road building, or readiness to care for the earth is totally neglected.

However, the worldview that has nurtured the development of science and the commitment of scientific technology to development is a worldview that believes that nature is other than God. It is not just a coincidence that the global spread of scientific technology has in most cases been preceded by the spread of the church and the biblical message.

This does not mean that everyone must become a Christian before the scientific revolution can take root. Not so. However, a society must be freed from the notions that the earth is god in order for authentic science to develop. The "salt" of Christian faith brings the gift of freedom from the gods of nature. Of course, some people discover this freedom from nature gods through atheistic philosophies.

God has created a real earth

The material world is not less real than spirit. It is not an illusion. Scientists can study the material world with confidence that they are exploring the mysteries of a real earth.

When the pioneer Christian missionary William Carey first arrived in Bengal in India a little over two centuries ago, he discovered considerable famine even though the region was rich in agricultural potential. He encountered a worldview that did not value agricultural development. The Hindu assumption that the material world is an illusion discouraged a serious attempt to develop agriculture.

Consequently, missionary Carey became a pioneer in challenging that worldview and providing models of authentic agricultural development; he is recognized even today as the father of modern Indian agriculture.[8]

God created a good earth

God's intention is that we enjoy and revel in the good gifts of creation. Yet, it is not a perfect world. Diseases such as malaria or droughts that destroy crops are obstacles to our enjoyment of creation.

We seek to understand God's creation so that we might address those aspects that threaten our well-being. For example, we develop drought-resistant maize or medicines that save lives from death through malaria. We rejoice and so does God in the eradication of diseases such as smallpox. These are examples of working together with God so that the earth might become not only good, but also very good.

However, we do not do research only so we can triumph over what threatens the well-being of people or nature. We also explore the earth just because it is good. We delight in discoveries of pure science, exploration of mountain peaks and ocean depths, or sending Rover to Mars. These are responses to the conviction that we live in a good and wonderful universe.

Notions that the earth and universe are evil, an illusion, or divinities do not encourage the exuberant spirit of discovery that must undergird authentic and creative scientific exploration and discovery. That spirit of discovery can only thrive in a worldview that believes the earth is good.

God sustains the earth.

God has not abandoned the earth or us. God sustains the earth in a manner consistent with the laws he has created. God is not capricious, changing creation laws on a whim. Consistent with his nature, the patterns and designs of creation are reliable and trustworthy. Therefore, our well-being demands that we live in a manner that is consistent with creation's patterns.

When TWA Flight 800 went down shortly after takeoff from John F. Kennedy Airport, we did not blame God. Rather a seventeen-month investigation commenced. In December 1997, the National Transportation Safety Board concluded its report by stating that the cause of the crash was an explosion in the center fuel tank.

The experts made recommendations to prevent such an accident in the future. They knew there is a reliable pattern in nature; hot fuel, enclosed oxygen, and a spark will cause an explosion. The proposed remedy: design planes so these ingredients of an explosion will not converge. We are responsible to discover and function in the patterns established in creation.

There was never any assumption by the investigators that God was responsible for the crash. In some societies that might have been the assumption, or that nature spirits, witchcraft, or fate determined the crash. However, the biblical view is that the earth functions reliably, for God is trustworthy. He creates and sustains his creation in a manner consistent with his trustworthy character. The manner in which the investigation of the crash proceeded is consistent with that biblical understanding.

"What about miracles?" we ask. "Don't miracles represent God intervening in the laws of creation?"

As far as I know, miracles in the Bible and the experience of the church happen in certain boundaries established by God's laws of creation. There are numerous accounts of crippled people being healed miraculously, both in the Bible and in modern times. However, I have not heard or read of any accounts of a leg that has been amputated growing back again. I do not doubt that God could create a new leg where one has been cut off. But that kind of miracle would be moving beyond the bounds of the laws of creation that God has put in place, laws that God himself has chosen to respect.

The miraculous healing of a cripple represents the multiplication of cells in the leg such that the broken, short, or warped leg becomes straight, strong, and normal. It seems God heals cripples, when he chooses to do so miraculously, through the multiplication of cells already in the leg of the cripple. But God does not choose to create brand new legs out of nothing. God expects us to honor the laws of creation just as he does.

As mentioned above, science can thrive only where there is confidence in the reliability of the laws of creation; Christians believe that the laws of creation are reliable because God sustains the earth in a trustworthy and noncapricious way.

People should care for and develop the good earth.

In a later chapter we will consider ways that we exploit and destroy the good earth. We note here, however, that God's first commands to humanity are the mandates to have children and develop the earth in a manner that reveals genuine care for the earth.

During my first visit to Albania after the collapse of communism, I was appalled at the economic and ecological disaster in that country despite being blessed with gifted people and bountiful natural resources. This tiny country had endured about fifty years of repressive atheism. I had many conversations, one with a physics professor.

He shared, "I am an atheist. I would like to be a believer, but what I hear you Christians say sounds like nonsense. My question is, "Imagine I have a tomato in my hand; what relationship does God have to the tomato?"

I responded, "The implications of the first chapter of the Bible are: God created the delicious tomato, care for the tomato, plant and cultivate the tomato, develop it into a better tomato, and enjoy the tomato!"

He exclaimed, "I can believe that! Please, send us Bible teachers."

The Earth Belongs to God

There is intense debate about the destructive dimensions of technology and the associated role of religion or Christian faith. Consequently many people are looking for other alternatives to religion. Ecologists remind us that we are part of the "web of life." When we relate destructively to the earth and other species, we are self-destructive. Others encourage us to embrace the notion that the earth is divine. They believe reverence for the earth as god will create in us the commitment to living harmoniously with the divine earth, and thereby we can resist the destructiveness of technology and selfish exploitation of nature.

I cannot address these concerns adequately in this brief book. My intention here is to simply present biblical faith with clarity. God created the earth; it is good; it belongs to God.

We are commanded to care for and develop the earth in a manner that blesses and sustains both creation and humanity. Exploitation of the earth is wrong: throwing plastic bags into the field, letting goats overgraze sahelian Africa, or poisoning the ground with toxic wastes is sinful and wrong. Biblical faith abhors the destruction and exploitation of the earth.

The biblical poet reminds us that "The earth is the Lord's, and everything in it, the world, and all who live in it" (Ps. 24:1). Let us care for the good earth. Let us be thankful. In millions of Christian households in societies and cultures around the world, believers thank God for food before eating their meals. All we eat comes from the good earth. We cultivate and plant, but it is the creation of God that brings forth the fruitfulness that provides us with the nourishment we need for life.

Let us live as good stewards of God's bounty. Let us develop the good earth in a manner that blesses the earth and humanity. Let us revel in its beauty.

• • •

Science continually surprises us with discoveries that reveal amazing things about creation. Imagine, for example, a microscopic worm with ninety-seven million chemical components.

All of this astonishing world is God's creation. Also astonishing is that God has entrusted the care of this good earth to us. What an amazing responsibility! There is a widespread notion that science and faith are enemies. It is thus surprising to find that biblical faith encourages and nurtures the development of scientific investigation and technology. But beware! When science turns against the good earth or humanity, it is wrong and contrary to God's intention. Developing the earth does not mean destroying or exploiting it; rather it means to care for the earth in a manner that blesses the earth and humanity as well.

Live thankfully! No wonder Christians thank God before they eat. Food is God's gift. So let us thank God, again and again, for food and for all God's surprising and wonderful gifts.

3

THE WISE ONES

Background Scripture: Genesis 1:26-31; 2:7, 15-25
Are they livestock or human?
Are they property or people?

These were the questions the Supreme Court of the United States of America debated in Steven Spielburg's film, *Amistad*.

Former U.S. President John Quincy Adams represented Cinque and his companions. These fifty-three slaves born in West Africa had staged an insurrection aboard the slave ship, *La Amistad*, in 1839.

The debate was momentous. The outcome threatened the stability of international relations between the U.S. and Spain. Southern states threatened civil war if La Amistad slaves were freed.

Adams argued from the Declaration of Independence that La Amistad Africans were created for freedom.

The Supreme Court, after intense and sometimes combative debate, and after thorough research of national and international law, made a determination. These wise and experienced judges declared that if the treaty with Spain applied to La Amistad, then the Africans were property, with no rights to freedom. However, since the treaty with Spain in relationship to slavery did not apply to the Amistad, these Africans were human and had all the rights to stage insurrection and gain freedom. So the intricacies of the treaty with Spain determined whether these people were livestock or human! How could a treaty between nations determine whether a people are livestock or human, property or people created for freedom?

The Amistad debate, which occurred a couple of decades before the American Civil War, went to the soul of a fundamental question: Who are we? "You are only animals!" expounded my graduate school anthropology professor as she paced back and forth across her lecture platform. Gesturing expansively she continued, "Scientific evidence proves that you have evolved from the primates. You are only intelligent animals."

As we jotted notes on this bit of scientific data, I thought, "In that case, why develop civilizations and cultures? Why the American Declaration of Independence? Why the developing global quest for human rights? Why not continue slavery?"

The human genus and specific epithet is called homosapiens, meaning human beings with wisdom. That wisdom is more than intelligence. What is this extra wisdom that characterizes humanity? Why do people, not animals, develop civilizations and cultures? Why do we yearn for human rights and freedoms?

The Great Debate

These questions are not trivial. The debate between creationists and evolutionary theory reveals the soul of these questions. Yet we often debate trivialities and miss the heart of the issues. My anthropology teacher, nevertheless, revealed a core struggle in the debate. What does it mean to be a person?

"Who are you?" I asked my third-year students in theology class at Lithuania Christian College. The class was deeply divided. In small groups the debate raged. Essays revealed the cleavage and the awareness of how significant the question is.

One student commented, "Marxism taught us that science has proved we are only biological creatures. I hope I am created in God's image, but I doubt that could be true."

The classroom debate was touched with pathos because everyone was aware that any discussion about human rights is ultimately based on the response to the question: who am I? The Soviet system that had entrapped Lithuania for some five decades took evolutionary theory to its ultimate conclusion since the person was only biology, the rights and dignity of the person were of no consequence.

For many weeks a confrontational debate raged between creationists and evolutionists in our local newspaper in Lancaster, Pennsylvania. Evolutionists argued from fossil evidence that life has developed over millions of years; the creationists declared that it all happened about 6,000 years ago. The creationists based their assertions primarily on biblical genealogies, and on the six creation days of Genesis 1. The evolutionists relied on radiocarbon dating and fossil evidence, data that the creationists tried to discredit.

The Bible says, "In the beginning God created. . . . " Would it not be wise to let the scientists explore when that beginning commenced, and the biblical scholars interpret the genealogies? By focusing on issues of time, both sides were evading several very fundamental differences between biblical faith and naturalistic evolutionary theory.

The debate in our hometown newspaper revealed the approach that some Christians take in relationship to evolutionary theory. There is much divergence among Christians on this issue, however. Some Christians, such as those in our local newspaper debate, totally reject evolution and take a literal approach to Genesis 1 and 2, including twenty-four-hour days for the creation of the world and animal and plant life.

Others avoid the issues by saying science and religion function in such different spheres that we should not try to reconcile the two; let science be science and religion be religion. Some Christians adopt the notion of theistic evolution; they accept that species have evolved, but believe that God brought about that evolution. We also note that in recent times, a cluster of scientists and Christian theologians are raising serious questions regarding fossil evidence supporting any notions of evolution from one species to another.

Whatever the outcome of the debate might be concerning the fossil records, there are fundamental differences between evolutionary theory and biblical faith. These differences move us beyond the kinds of debate that raged in our local newspaper or that is described in the alternatives noted above. The differences are profoundly significant for our understanding of human life, as well as all other forms of life.

I highlight three basic and irreconcilable differences between naturalistic evolutionary theory and biblical faith.

Did God create the species?

Alternatively, have the species evolved through natural selection? The Genesis 1 creation account is obviously based on careful observations and declares that God created the plants and animals "according to their kinds" (Gen. 1:11-12, 20-26).

There is abundant evidence of minuscule evolution (change and adaptation) in species. Such adaptation is not contrary to biblical faith. However, as I understand it, biblical faith insists that the Creator formed the heavens, earth, and living things. These phenomena are not created by impersonal minerals, chemicals, a big bang, or primordial goo. Personal intelligence is responsible. "By faith we understand that the universe was formed at God's command. . . " (Heb. 11:3).

Books galore have been written on evidence fossils provide both for and against the evolution from one species to another. Much of the debate occurs in the scientific community itself. One leader of the debate is Harvard University palaeobiologist, Stephen Jay Gould, who argues that evolution from one species to another cannot be demonstrated by fossil evidence.

In recent years a University of California law professor, Phillip Johnson, has launched a movement to discredit evolutionary theory; he also bases his confrontation on the fossil evidence. Johnson uses his legal skills to demonstrate that evidence from the fossils does not support a theory of evolution from one species to a new species. That does not happen in the biological world as we observe it today, and neither does the fossil evidence support such notions. Johnson asserts that if the evidence for and against the theory of evolution were presented as a legal case in a court of law, the jury would rule against evolution.[1]

Whatever the case might be, biblical faith is clear: God is the creator of the heavens and earth and all forms of life. Theories of naturalistic evolution of life are not biblical.

Are people only animals?

Indeed, human beings are mammals. In fact, in the biblical account they were created on the sixth day of creation when the other mammals were created (Gen. 1:26,27). A few paragraphs later we read that God formed the man from the dust of the earth (Gen. 2:7). We are mammals formed from the earth. The chimpanzee dies; so do we. We are biological creatures.

My anthropology professor was right in saying that we were animals. However, she included another word: "only." Biblical faith objects totally! The human mammal is much more than an animal. We are created in God's image. God has breathed the breath of life into us (Gen. 2:7).

No other animals are created in God's image, only human beings. We are special. Human beings are both in continuity with the animals and in otherness from the animals.

The otherness from animals is far more profound than intelligence alone. In fact, in some narrowly defined ways some animals are more clever than humans. For example, recently BBC news reported a startling scientific finding. A species of sea turtles hatch in certain streams entering the Atlantic from the West Coast of Africa. The young turtles then swim many months across the Atlantic to Brazil, and later swim back to Africa to hatch their own young in the same stream where they were born.

Investigators believe these turtles' brains contain the capability of reading the earth's electromagnetic field, which is the guiding mechanism they use to navigate their ocean voyages. Try that, if you think you are smarter than a turtle!

However, neither the turtles nor any other animals create cultures and civilizations. People on the other hand are wise beings. God has breathed his wisdom and his spirit into us. And because we are created in God's image, people create cultures and civilizations.

Is survival of the fittest the law of nature?

If, as theory of evolution states, human beings and our societies are only the evolutionary extension of the animal world, and if natural selection through survival of the fittest is the law of nature, then the suppression of the weak is mandated and inevitable. Evolutionary theory is cruel.

Applied to the social sciences, the theory of evolution has nurtured racist ideologies. Hitler embraced the theory in his Nazi ideology and pulled the world into World War II. According to his ideology, the Aryan race was at the evolutionary pinnacle. It was the only race fit to rule all other races. Eradication of some less fit races was necessary to preserve the earth for the most fit races.

Marxists in the Soviet Union also embraced the theory of natural selection and the survival of the fittest. In their ideology, the superior people who were fit to rule were the laborers or proletariat. The leaders of the proletariat slaughtered tens of millions of people. Members of these Nazi and Soviet societies could not critique the ideologies because they were "scientific." The natural selection of the best was the unalterable truth of nature and society.

It is surprising how sharply and irreconcilably biblical faith parts ways with any "might makes right" ideology. In astonishing contrast to evolutionary theory, the Christian Way is empowered by the suffering love and vulnerability of God. The power center of the universe is not the power of the fittest, but

As image of God beings, people are *homo sapiens*, the wise ones. Yet whenever we turn away from our Creator and seek a wisdom that is contrary to his nature, we are inclined to become a foolish people prone to committing evil. The assumption that might makes right is a startling example of a foolishness that has led whole civilizations into a taste of hell in the twentieth century. The notion that might makes right is in opposition to our Creator, who reveals that love that suffers, makes right. True wisdom embraces our Creator's love and gives of oneself in loving service for the other.

However, some will object, "In nature, might does make right; the survival of the fittest does apply." It is true that in nature, the weaker animals do not survive the winter; the stronger animals do. These principles of natural selection help to keep animal and plant life in healthy equilibrium. Nevertheless, even in this natural system, God has put in place protections for the weak; for example, foolish and vulnerable rock conies live in caves in the rocks!

In the Bible, cruelty to animals is abhorrent. Trees likewise are to be preserved and not uselessly destroyed.

If God was concerned about the well-being of plants and animals, the Bible reveals even greater concern for people. Again and again the biblical writers proclaimed God's concern for the well-being of the widows, orphans, poor, and the strangers (refugees). When modern people apply natural selection to human societies, it is an atrocious distortion of the nature of God and his plan for humanity.

Even the malformed baby who will never be able to walk is a precious being created in God's image and needs to be cherished and cared for. This is because that vulnerable baby is also a God-like being.

Godlike Beings!

At an eastern Australian barbecue in New Castle, a woodsman described his love for Australia's wilderness, "I don't need any religion; that stuff is irrelevant. The woods are enough for me."

I responded, "God might surprise you."

"Never! I will never believe; the woods are enough for me."

I persisted, "Imagine walking in the outback enjoying the wonder of it all, and knowing that the Creator delights when you enjoy it with him. Wouldn't that be a great joy?"

"Don't try to convert me!" he exclaimed.

"Relax," I suggested. "I can't convert you. That decision is between you and God."

That conversation was a revelation of two ways to walk through life's woods. We can enjoy the creation while ignoring the Creator, or we can celebrate the wonder of being daughters and sons of God and live in joyful thanksgiving to our Creator.

The implications of being created in God's image are startling. We will explore several of these surprises of what it means to be Godlike people.

God's Qualities and Our Response

Let us consider several of God's qualities and ways that our Godlike image enables us to create cultures and civilizations.

God communicates; we develop and speak languages.

God creates; we create artifacts, such as building houses, making tools, or weaving clothing.

God is righteous; we have a moral conscience and develop systems of right and wrong.

God chooses; we develop systems to reward or punish people for the choices they make.

God is personal; we carry an awareness of the dignity of the person. Every human on earth has a name. We create schools to help the person develop.

God fellowships; we develop societies and social systems to nurture our fellowship and relationships with one another. We also need fellowship with God.

God is eternal; we develop burial systems and religious practices that recognize the extension of human life beyond biological death.

God is Trinity (diversity, complementarity, and unity); we celebrate diversity. One of the most joyous moments in the rituals of a society is a wedding, the affirmation and celebration of the complementary, diversity, and union of male and female.

God works and rests enjoying his labor; We also work, tilling the earth, building homes, cooking food, and other forms of labor. Societies everywhere also have times of rest and celebration enjoying the fruit of their labor.

Respect for the Person

The total person is created in God's image. It is not the mind alone. Not the body alone. Not the spirit or soul alone. The whole person is created in God's image. That conviction is the foundation for the biblical respect for the dignity and freedom of the person.

Respect for the person was the focus of a visit by twenty Chinese government leaders from Sichuan Province to our community in the United States. They asked for someone to talk with them during their dinner hour on the topic of "Ways the Christian Faith Influences American Culture." The hosts invited me to give a half-hour address speaking through an interpreter.

I said, "Most church buildings have a steeple. That is a sign that our creator God is other than creation. But he speaks. The preacher stands beneath the steeple proclaiming God's Word to those who have gathered for worship.

"What does God say? One thing he says is that we are created in his own image. That means that every person has dignity and significance. For that reason we Christians encourage our government to respect human rights.

"Every person on earth is equally God's image: Chinese, African, or Caucasian, children or the elderly. Both man and woman are equally God's image."

At that moment, spontaneous Mandarin debate burst across the room. It seemed to me they were all talking at once.

Man and Woman in God's Image

Our guests were intrigued to discover that woman and man are equally created in God's image. In traditional China the male has greater value than the female. In modern times the value of the male has become especially evident. Due to population pressure, the government requires that couples bear only one child. With the one-child policy, many parents abort the female fetuses. They want a boy baby!

In radical departure from such values, the biblical account is that both the man and the woman are equally created in God's image. Both are equally precious. Both have equal dignity and deserve equal respect. This concept is revolutionary for all societies, and in fact Christians themselves do not always live according to these principles. There are practices and attitudes in some Christianized societies that suppress women and communicate the notion that men are more valuable than women.

We recognize, of course, that the Bible was developed in male-centered cultures. The Genesis vision of male and female being equal in God's image is not a challenge to only modern cultural norms; it was quite disturbing in biblical times as well.

This is because male and female made equally in God's image reveals that God revels in diversity and complementarity. In a later chapter I discuss God as Trinity. Here I just note that in God diversity and complementarity are integrated in oneness.

As people we participate in one humanity, yet in that humanity there is the diversity and complementarity of male and female (Gen. 1:27; 2:21-25). The continuation of the human race depends on that diversity.

Male and female diversity are fundamental to our humanity as the image of God-creatures. God as Trinity is not a homogenous oneness. There is diversity, complementarity, and fellowship in God himself, and we as male and female reflect diversity with complementarity.

This biblical theology of diversity in the unity of God is one with theological significant implications for the conversation taking place in many churches concerning homosexuality. In some churches there is considerable debate concerning the appropriate Christian response to persons who have same-sex partners. This debate is especially intense in Western societies and church.

The nature of God (theology) should be at the center of the discussion about homosexuality. Here are three examples of ways theology can contribute to the discernment.

First, God loves us, redeems us, and saves us. What does it mean for the church to be loving and redemptive to people involved in homosexual relations?

Second, God expresses his diversity in unity in loving complementary relations. What does a homosexual relationship indicate concerning the unity and diversity of male and female both being created in God's image?

Third, because God loves, he creates new life, including human life. We observe that in the marriage relationship the diversity and unity of male and female is life giving; a homosexual relationship is not life-creating.

Marriage and Singleness

The essence of marriage, then, is the one-flesh union of a man and a woman expressing the union of their diverse creation in God's image. (Gen. 2:24). This surprise is uniquely biblical.

Unless a society has been influenced by ideas from biblical revelation, a prevailing perception in non-Christianized traditional societies is that the woman in the marriage is like a garden. Her husband possesses her so that he might sow seed in his garden, so that she can conceive and bear children.[2] Alternatively, the woman, especially the mistress, may be viewed as the provider of sexual pleasure for the man.

"No! No!" biblical faith exclaims. The woman is not a garden, nor is she created solely for the sexual pleasure of the man. She is created in God's image, just as her husband is. The soul of a marriage is the one-flesh union, a covenant communion between equals (Gen. 2:20-25). Sexual pleasure in marriage is equally significant and should be cherished by both the husband and the wife (1 Cor. 7:4-5). He seeks to minister to her need for sexual pleasure and she seeks to minister to his. Of course, the husband and wife have different roles in the home, but both are equally people in God's image.

Children are not mentioned in any biblical description of the meaning of marriage. They are a blessing, but not essential to the soul of a marriage. However, God does command us to "be fruitful and increase in number" (Gen. 1:28). Married couples should cherish children if their home is blessed with them.

Divorce is not in harmony with the image of God in unity that marriage represents. Divorce is tragic and painful; it is like driving a wedge into the unity of God. It is a violation of our true humanity as male and female image of God beings.

Recently my wife and I visited a home where the husband/father had left the home many years before. We discovered that the pain of that separation was still present. The gift of God's grace and love can be a healing ointment creating beauty and new life where there has been such a deep wound. For many years my wife has ministered to divorcees; God's grace does touch grieving and disappointed lives with joy and hope.

Polygamy is also a violation of the one-flesh marriage union. I have lived in societies for many years that practiced polygamy. If the essence of marriage is children, polygamy thrives. However, polygamy is a violation of our humanity if the essence of marriage is the one-flesh union of a man and a woman equally created in God's image. An African friend once told me, "In polygamy the-one flesh union between husband and wife is dead, completely dead!"

Wholesome relations between women and men mean that singleness is an option. Complementarity of male and female does not require sexual union. We experience our fullest humanity in a right relationship with our Creator and with one another; those relationships enrich singleness.

Woman and man, equally created in God's image: this is one of the good news surprises of the Christian Way. Biblical faith invites an astonishing new creation in male-female relationships.

Develop the Good Earth

The previous chapter addressed human responsibility to develop the good earth. We will not elaborate further here except to note that as image-of-God-creatures we have received the capability and responsibility to care for as well as to develop the good earth.

It is noteworthy that although Islam believes in God as creator, Islam does not accept that people are created in God's image. It follows, then, that in Islam it is God who names the animals and teaches Adam their names. In contrast, in the Bible it is Adam who names the animals (Gen. 2:19,20). We who follow this biblical teaching have that responsibility. In Islam God instructs Adam and his descendants how to be caretakers of the earth. The surprise of the Christian Way is that God entrusts us with that responsibility.

Being created in God's image has astonishing implications. for culture and civilization, human rights, marriage, male and female relations, and development and care of the earth. Truly if we are made in God's image, what a privilege and responsibility it is to be human!

One Human Family

Adam and Eve are the first parents of every person on earth. This means that we are all one human family. Although we cluster in groups, such as family, language, or nation, we are all one humanity.

My parents had five children. Although we are very different from one another, we are loyal to each other and would never think of doing something to hurt or harm a member of our family. We care for each other. It is important to recognize that in a very fundamental way, the same should be true of our relationship to every person on Earth; each of us is a brother and sister, because we all descend from those very same first parents.

Fellowship with God

The most remarkable surprise of being created in God's image is that we are created for fellowship with God. We can know God, commune with God, walk through life enjoying a joyous relationship with God. In fact, Jesus invites us to discover that God is our Father, our Daddy.

We will explore the joys of knowing God as our loving Father in the chapters that follow. It is the abiding astonishment of the Christian Way that the God who created this vast universe longs for us to know him as our Father, our loving parent. That is the ultimate meaning and surprise of being created in God's image.

• • •

When our first grandchild, Chloe, was born we immediately drove the sixty miles from our home to the city of Baltimore in Maryland to welcome her. What a delight to see her; we took pictures, held her, and thanked God for her. And she looked like her Grandmother. Even today, several years after that birth, if I want to fill Grace's soul with delight, I just comment, "Chloe really does look like you!"

God's delight was even greater when he created the first human couple. He exclaimed with joy and elation, "Ah, very good! They really are like me!" And the delight is reciprocal. It is wonderful and astonishing to know that we are created in God's image.

I enjoy jogging in the early morning, especially through the Lithuanian woods near Kretingos. It is a time to especially enjoy being created in God's image. "Wow!" I share with God as I jog along the pathways in the woods. "Thank you for creating me in your image! Thanks, my Father, for creating these woods, birds, air, and clouds, that I enjoy so much. What a delight to know you as my Father!"

4

THE ENEMY INVADES

Background Scripture: Genesis 3:1-4:9; Revelation 22:1-3

An army of green men from Mars had invaded earth!

My grandmother told me about the day she heard this announcement on the radio. The news reporters somberly described the invaders landing in a field in New Jersey; they began to attack and occupy the nearby town. These soldiers were horrible looking green creatures.

Grandmother was terrified. Panic swept across the United States. People raced to the banks to get their money to hide their wealth from the green Martian invaders.

Eventually people were informed that the invasion from Mars was fiction. The radio was playing a radio play by H.G. Wells about a Martian invasion. Those who had tuned into the story late were fooled by its realism. There were no Martians.

However, the arrival of Halley's Comet in 1910 was real. Astronomers predicted the earth would pass through Halley's tail and might be incinerated. Thousands of couples living together unmarried rushed to churches for weddings. Fire engines stood by the Bank of England in London for any eventuality.

For many years, accounts of UFOs such as flying saucers or cigar-shaped, airborne behemoths have captivated us. The US National Aeronautic and Space Administration invests millions of dollars listening for possible signals from beings from elsewhere who might want to contact Earth. This is high drama.

The First Invasion

The first alien invader has led an insurrection against God our righteous creator. It is God who gives life; the alien declaration of independence against God, our life giver, has introduced death and destruction among humanity and on the good earth.

The alien invaders on television are mostly spooky looking with little horns or strangely crinkled skin. They usually make fearful demands and threats and sometimes capture people and take them to remote planets. However, the first invader was not like that; he appeared as a concerned friend, a wise serpent. The invader invited Adam and Eve to experience freedom and wisdom by becoming independent from their Creator.

Freedom and choice

Who is this alien invader? Where did he come from? What were his intentions?

To understand the mind of this alien invader we need to understand the phenomenon of choice in God and in the universe. Choice provides the possibility for goodness. Choice also allows the opportunity for evil. We will explore the relation between choice and evil, but first we need to look at the relationship of God to the presence of evil.

If God is good, why evil?

We cannot avoid this question: If God is good and all powerful, why is there evil?

First, a clarification. Tragedy is different than evil. Earthquakes might bring tragedy. Christians as well as the biblical writers struggle with the "why" of such tragedies. Is tragedy the judgment of God on people for their sinfulness? Is God trying to get people's attention? Do such calamities just happen without any need to theologize about the reasons? Tragedies do demonstrate that this is not a perfect earth. The biblical book of Job struggles with these questions and so do we.

However, evil is different than tragedy. Evil is the personal choice to destroy what is good. Most human suffering by far around the world comes from evil, not tragedy. Biblical writers, Christian theologians, and philosophers struggle with the paradox of a good God and evil in our world.

The thrust of the Bible is that evil enters because of our personal and collective choice to turn away from God, or just ignore God, our good and righteous creator. We are not puppets. We are responsible. The choice between evil and good has been present since our creation.

Decision time!

God is the source of goodness. His goodness requires personal choice. God is good; he makes choices. Likewise we humans created in God's image have personal choice. Animals function primarily through instinct; nature largely defines their behavior. Animals cannot choose between good and evil. Humans, however, can; we do make those kinds of choices.

Humans are not puppets with no responsibility for their conduct. That is why every society has courts or councils that determine punishment for offenders. The foundation on which societies develop systems of punishment and rewards is the universal belief that human beings are responsible for their actions.

Human beings are personal. We are beings of choice. We are responsible for the choices we make.

Angels and other spiritual beings

Perhaps there are planets in various regions of the universe where personal beings reside who are like humans with material bodies; we do not know.

However, the Bible does mention personal spiritual beings with nonmaterial bodies that we normally are not capable of seeing, who are also beings of choice. I use the word "normally" advisedly. Both in the Bible and today there are reports by persons who describe seeing an angel or a spirit who appears and then disappears.

God created angels or spirits as well as humans with the ability to accept God's delightful invitation to live in fellowship with God in bringing about goodness and righteousness (Heb. 1:6,7).

Insurrection in the heavens

But John, the author of Revelation, saw a vision of rebellion against God in heaven. Satan and a host of angels declared their independence from God (Rev. 12:7-9). We know nothing about the nature of the battle between the hosts of angels loyal to God and those in rebellion, except that in John's vision the angels were thrown down to earth. Revelation also assures us that although the insurrection continues, the victory of God over the rebellious angels is already underway and God has promised that the final victory is assured. John refers to Satan, the leader of the rebellion, as "that ancient serpent" (Rev. 12:9).

Except in Revelation, Satan or the Devil is not a prominent theme in the Bible; however, an awareness of the presence and evil influence of Satan is recognized occasionally in addition to the Revelation scriptures. For example, Satan tried to seduce Job to turn away from God (Job 1:6-12, 2:1-7). Jesus, likewise was very aware of Satan's deceptions.

The Biblical references to Satan lead us to believe that the enemy invader of planet Earth is Satan. He is the commanding general of the hosts of angels who are in rebellion against God. The battle between good and evil rages throughout the universe. A Cambridge University Professor, the late C.S. Lewis, commented, "There is no neutral ground in the universe: every square inch and every split second is claimed by God and counterclaimed by Satan."[1]

This vision of Satan's rebellion against God appears in Revelation, the last book of the Bible. However, humankind's rebellion is recorded in Genesis, the first book.

The Declaration of Independence

God placed the tree of knowledge of good and evil in the Garden of Eden. He commanded Adam and Eve to not eat the fruit of that tree. However, the serpent objected. Who is this serpent? Is he that "ancient serpent"—Satan—that is described in the last book of the Bible? Some traditionalists do believe the serpent is indeed Satan, as shown in Wisdom 2:24, which was written by Jewish believers between the Old and New Testament Scriptures.

The serpent asserted that God was keeping something good from Adam and Eve, "For God knows that when you eat of it your eyes will be opened, and you will be like God, knowing good and evil" (Gen. 3:5).

Eve took the fruit and then gave some to Adam and he also ate. They ate because they saw that the fruit was . . . good for food and pleasing to the eye, and also desirable for gaining wisdom. . ." (Gen. 3:6). Immediately their eyes were opened. They knew they were naked. Their innocence was gone. They sewed aprons of fig leaves. They hid in the bushes hoping God would not discover them.

The Tree of Knowledge

What is the meaning of the tree of the knowledge of good and evil? Why did the serpent urge Adam and Eve to eat that fruit? Why did eating of that fruit create such guilt and shame?

The tree is a symbol of our source of understanding good and evil. The tree is an expression of creation, of nature. The symbolizes our looking to creation for guidance concerning good and evil. But creation should not have the final authority over our lives; God should be recognized as the final authority.

"Nature's laws" should not be our arbitrator of good and evil. During the twentieth century, political ideologies have brought a taste of hell to earth as believers have sought to build systems of good and evil based on "natural law" (Marxism and Nazism). The American Declaration of Independence is based on "self-evident" truths, another way of expressing natural law. Has that moral foundation in natural law contributed to the American readiness to lead the world in the arms race? The patriotism of Japanese Shinto nature worship brought unspeakable calamity to vast regions of Asia. No natural tree in our garden of life should have the authority to reveal good and evil; that is God's responsibility.

There is no choice in natural laws; neither does nature provide for good and evil alternatives. When people turn to nature worship they discover such benign gifts as harvests, but eventually also the terrifying face of the leopard that my Tanzanian friend once worshiped (Chapter 2). The "law" of natural selection that is a cornerstone of the theory of evolution is cruel.

Nature cannot be an adequate foundation for determining goodness. This is true if one worships nature as divinity. It is equally true if one believes that nature is self-sustained, impersonal natural laws. In either case nature is not a valid basis for determining right and wrong human behavior.

The Terrence Malick award-winning film, *A Thin Red Line*, mentioned earlier, is a powerful insight into the moral confusion of nature veneration. This Guadalcanal wartime film provides probing insight into the nature-based morality of postmodernism as well as the New Age Movement. There is no moral center, although there is a keen awareness that good and evil are intermingling on the battlefield. From what source does good and evil grow, and how does one discern between the two? That is the perplexity and confusion of the soldiers for whom nature was their primary frame of reference.

Adam and Eve were deeply ashamed for what they had done. They had placed themselves and that tree at the center of their world, instead of God. They had declared their independence of God. If they needed moral guidance, nature, not God, would provide that guidance. In their self-centered confusion they tried to hide from God, crouching behind the bushes.

The source of evil

The source of evil is humanity's declaration of independence from God. Although societies everywhere recognize the problem of wrongdoing, only in biblical faith is the core cause identified as our choice to reject the authority of God.

Some of my college theology students object, "We have never rejected God. In fact, we have never met God. We don't have a clue whether there is a God, so how can we reject God?"

If I enter the college classroom and begin to speak, but a group of students at the back of the room totally ignores me, paying no attention to what I am trying to say, that is rejection. Likewise, ignoring God who is everywhere and who is attempting to get the attention of each one of us is also rejection.

Evil entered human history when our first parents made two decisions that demonstrated their choice to reject God. First, they decided to embrace nature (the tree of the knowledge of good and evil) for their moral guidance, rather than God. Second, they chose to place themselves instead of their Creator at the center of their universe.

Those decisions to look to nature rather than to God's revelation for their sense of right and wrong and to place themselves rather than God at the center are the source of sin and evil for Adam and Eve and for all of us.

Other faiths and ideologies sidestep this biblical core understanding of the root causes of evil.

Hinduism blames ignorance.

Buddhism cites the allure of wrong desires.

African Traditional Religions decry evil spirits and malevolent ancestors as the originators of evil.

The American dream points to the absence of democracy.

Islam speaks of mistakes.

Marxism blames the bourgeois (owners of property and wealth).

Different schools of psychology blame environment, heredity, hang-ups over parents, or the id (repressed subconscious).

Some New Age gurus blame our modern distancing from nature and the natural inner spirit.

However, the Bible sings from a different sheet of music; we experience sinfulness personally and collectively because we turn away from God and choose to live independently of God.

Stubborn sinfulness

Adam and Eve are the first parents of all of us. They were the first to declare their independence from God. We sometimes exclaim, "Like father, like son." That is true. The Adam and Eve spirit of independence from our Creator has infected everyone of us and all human societies. Likewise the inclination to sinfulness lies deep in every human soul.

Let me give an example. God is always truthful. Yet when a student acquaintance did a survey of college students, and asked the question whether they would tell a lie if it served to protect them from an inconvenience, with rare exception every student said, "Of course!"

I have stressed the biblical insistence that sinfulness has entered our experience through choice. The reality is, however, that the infection of sinfulness runs so deeply in our spirits that our will is also infected. It is rather like an alcoholic who is entrapped in excessive drinking. His will is paralyzed.

It is for this reason that God does not stand neutrally on the sidelines and watch us struggle. No, God actively looks for us and seeks to empower our will to say yes to his call to turn from our lives of independence from God and live in fellowship and obedience to him. This is the drama of the Bible we will explore in the next chapters.

We turn now to a more thorough exploration of sin.

Sin

Modern psychiatry has avoided dealing with the phenomenon of evil; that is the conclusion of psychiatrist M. Scott Peck. In his book, *People of the Lie*, Peck seeks to address that avoidance. He describes persons who are evil; they destroy those around them through their attitudes.[2]

According to Peck, there is a consistent pattern in these destructive attitudes:
- blaming others for personal failure;
- intolerance to criticism;

- excessive concern with public image;
- deviousness.

The evil person perceives himself as his own ultimate authority and therefore never needs to repent. The evil person might be respected and professional, yet he is destructive.

One does not need to read the Bible to gain glimpses of sin. Peck's case studies are revelations of the evil inclinations in all of us. As I read his four descriptions of the evil person, I admit that all four inclinations abide in my soul. The daily newspaper is also an ample revelation of our sinful inclinations. So are our neighborhoods. Sinfulness is a biblical truth that has irrefutable evidence; if you are not persuaded, read your local newspaper.

Genesis 3 reveals profound insight in describing the universal consequences of our declaration of independence from God. We note ten of those consequences here.

1. People in societies everywhere experience shame or guilt. We all know that we have fallen short of who we really should be. We identify with Adam and Eve whose eyes were opened to who they really were, and they felt shame (3:7-10).

Societies develop devices to deal with shame or guilt. Animal sacrifices are a universal response to shame or guilt among primal religions. Muslims will say extra prayers. Some Christians might do penance. Buddhists will give to the monks in their quest for merit and forgiveness. Adam and Eve made aprons and hid in the bushes (3:7-8).

2. The aprons of fig leaves are a camouflage hiding the real person. We try to hide our true selves, our nakedness. Our cultures become our camouflage. Instead of meeting one another as authentic people, we meet dressed in our cultures. The clothing we wear, the degrees we flaunt, the jobs we do, or the families we come from become our fig leaf aprons. We evaluate people on the basis of culture; we avoid meeting in authentic person-to-person relationships.[3] I will describe two examples.

First, during the 1991 Gulf War I heard one American military officer refer to the Iraqi army as the enemy and a snake. Although thousands of Iraqis were killed in the war, I heard some commentators say that only a handful of people was killed. They were referring to the Americans killed. For these reporters, the Iraqis had ceased being people; their Iraqi fig leaf aprons disqualified them from being considered as human beings.

Second, in Rwanda the conflict between Hutu and Tutsi is influenced by cows. During the French colonial era the administration wanted to have a clear way to distinguish between the predominantly agricultural Hutu and the more pastoral Tutsi. So the colonial administration determined that any family with five or more cows was Tutsi. Those with fewer cows were Hutu. The society was divided between the less than five cows people and the more than four cows people. Cows became the cultural "leaves" that deepened divisions in Rwandan society and contributed to the genocidal war.

3. *Adam and Eve tried to hide from God.* They crouched behind the bushes (3:8-10). People everywhere develop techniques as they attempt to hide from their Creator. In Chapter 2, I mentioned an academic hiding-bush that a college professor described; believing in God would require reconciliation with his father, so rather than believe, he used so-called academic sophistication to justify his atheism.

Religion is one of the favorite ways people try to hide from God. During his years in a Nazi prison camp, the German theologian, Dietrich Bonhoeffer, discovered that most often it was easier to have authentic conversations concerning God with nonreligious people than with the religious. That surprise led him in a quest for a religionless Christianity.[4] Bonhoeffer was killed before he had the opportunity to develop his ideas, yet it seems he was observing that Jesus Christ calls us to follow him; he does not call us to embrace a religion.

Religions do not necessarily lead us closer to God; the religious person might actually be hiding from God. However, he uses his piety, theology, or religious ritual to pretend that he loves God.

In the New Testamen, the Apostle Paul addressed such concerns in the church in Galatia (Gal. 3:1-3, 4:8-10). This church was departing from God yet becoming increasingly religious. Paul insisted that God, not religion, saves us.

4. *Instead of taking responsibility for our choices, we blame others.* Adam blamed Eve and God. Eve blamed the serpent (3:12-13). We also project our guilt onto others.

5. *God told Eve there would be enmity between her and the serpent* (3:14-15). Eve would live in fear that evil would destroy her and her family. Instead of living in freedom, she was inclined to succumb to the serpent's wiles and the deceptions of other spirits that are in rebellion against God. Multitudes of societies live in fear of evil spiritual powers.

6. *Eve will give birth to children in greatly increased pain* (3:16). This refers to child birth, but probably also to the pain of alienation in parent and child relationships. My wife has been a hospital chaplain. She grieved over the many elderly who told her that their children never visit; their families had experienced broken relations. Instead of intergenerational harmony, many families experience intergenerational strife.

7. *Adam will dominate his wife and she will acquiesce* (3:16). Rather than the precious complementarity of man and woman equally created in God's image, the relations between the sexes are touched with destructiveness. During the mid-twentieth century there were anthropological case studies describing societies with harmony between the sexes or where women provided family leadership in a harmonious manner. Those studies are now discredited.

Every society reveals alienation between men and women. The social systems we create enable the man to dominate and require the woman to acquiesce.[5]

This does not refer to the appropriate differences in roles between men and women, or different roles in leadership responsibilities. Rather, it refers to men dominating women. Male domination of females was not and is not God's intention; however, in our sinfulness a pattern of domination tends to prevail in societies around the world.

8. *The land will be cursed because of Adam.* Thorns and thistles will grow (3:17-18). Instead of caring for the good earth and developing it, humans curse the earth and its creatures by mistreating creation. For example, cotton-growing estates in vast regions of the southeastern United States have ruined millions of acres of fertile soil. Instead of fertility, "thistles" grow.

In the northwestern United States, atomic energy and military plants have poisoned streams with "thistles" of atomic waste. We destroy species, treasures created by God to enrich our lives and bless the good earth. We live in alienation with the good earth instead of in responsible harmony with creation.

9. *We are alienated from the goodness of work.* God's first command to Adam and Eve was to work; "fill the earth and subdue it." Work is good. Work is a core dimension of being created in God's image. However, in turning away from God the goodness of work has become drudgery (3:19).

We may seek to avoid work or use work to exploit ourselves or creation. Instead of experiencing work as a blessing, we turn it into a "sweat shop" for ourselves and others.

10. *Adam and Eve experienced death.* Death summarizes all the expressions and consequences of sinfulness. Death is the consequence of declaring independence from the source of Life—God. Death is separation from fullness of life.

As time went on, Adam and Eve met a ghastly revelation of the depth of death that had ensnared them and their family. God blessed Adam and Eve with children. Cain was the firstborn and then his brother Abel was born. Jealousy took root in Cain's heart against his brother and Cain killed Abel. Murder occurred in the first human family (4:1-8).

The psychoanalyst Sigmund Freud also believed something dark and terrible happened in the first human family. He believed the sons killed and ate their father.[6] In the Bible the primal murder did happen but involved brother against brother.

The root of this murder was Cain's decision to exclude his brother. Earlier we observed that the cultural fig leaves we wear can become the basis for choices people of different cultures make to exclude each other. But in the account of Cain and Abel, the exclusion is between siblings. Excluding any person or any people from our loving concern is contrary to the Spirit of God and is the tap root that nurtures murder and warfare.

The Tree of Life

God sent Adam and Eve from the luscious Garden of Eden prepared especially for them as their first home (Gen. 3:23-24). There was the tree of life in that Garden. In their sinfulness they could not eat of that tree until God himself had provided a way for them to be redeemed (rescued) from their sinfulness.

In the last chapter of the Bible we discover another description of the tree of life appearing at the climax of human history; however, in that vision all people are welcome to eat its leaves and fruit (Gen. 3:22-24; Rev. 22:1-3). This means that at the end of the Bible we discover that in the grand conclusion of history the tragedy of the Garden of Eden is reversed forever.

The tree of life is a picture of the hope woven through the Bible. We will explore that hope in the next chapter. The tree represents a promise, the promise of God that love and righteousness will prevail over evil. God invites us to live in hope anchored to God's promises and the many signs that he is working for good. The tree of life is already flourishing among us!

• • •

I detest nasty surprises, like this one.

One bitterly cold dark night in December, I ran out of fuel on a remote stretch of expressway between Klaipeda and Vilnius in Lithuania. I have driven hundreds of thousands of miles in many countries in different parts of the world, and I should know better. I was astonished at my stupidity and irresponsible choices that night that led to this horrible predicament.

That was not the kind of surprise I enjoy. It was a terribly embarrassing surprise. It was dangerous. It was very cold, about 15 degrees Fahrenheit or minus 10 degrees Celsius. The nearest town was fifty kilometers away. What a dreadful surprise.

Our sinfulness is like that. We are embarrassed. Students in my religions or theology classes in Africa, America, or Lithuania, or in Asian and European seminars that I have taught, sometimes claim blandly that it just isn't true. My Muslim, secular, Buddhist, or Hindu friends chide the notion that we are sinful. We are inclined to deny sin.

Yet we all know that deep in our souls there is indeed a nasty surprise lurking in the shadows. Sinfulness is in us. The most pious people I know sometimes jolt me with their accidental revelations of sinfulness: Gossip about a friend or an unforgiving bitter spirit. Although we try, we really can't hide the secret,

It might be a surprise to know that the first contact and invasion has already happened. An alien arrived with a message especially for our first parents. This alien promised that if they would receive his message, the wisdom of homo sapiens would increase significantly. He advised that a declaration of independence from God, their creator, was necessary to achieve full human potential. even from our friends. We are sinful.

That night on the expressway I prayed. I asked my Father for help. Within minutes a car stopped on the opposite side of the expressway. The people in that auto had not seen my car; it was too dark. I ran across the four lanes and told them of my plight. They drove me twenty kilometers to the nearest gas station and later returned me to my car and saw me on my way.

That is the nature of God. He does not abandon us in our irresponsibility. He goes many kilometers out of his way, as it were, to help us.

Although our sinfulness might be a nasty surprise, God's eagerness to save us from our plight is even more surprising. God cruises the expressway of our life, and delights to stop with fuel for all who cry out, "God, I have been stupid; I need help!"

5

THE INTERCEPTION

Background Scripture: Isaiah 9:6-7; Matthew 1:21-22

God has run an interception to block Satan and his plans! In fact, God has declared war against all the powers of sin and death. He is standing in the midst of the battle; he doesn't stand in some safe bunker giving commands to his soldiers who die in battle. No! God is also wounded and suffers with us in the battle. But he never retreats. He intends victory; God loves us totally, and he is committed to rescuing people everywhere from the evil, death, and brokenness that entrap us.

However, most people have no idea God is interceding and has chosen to stand with us in all of life's struggles. That was true of the lonely old Ba'ila woman I describe below; she had no clue God was present. She thought she needed to find God; alas, she did not realize God has already entered our pathos.

Listen to her story. Perhaps this is also your story, walking through life wondering where God can be found.

Many generations ago, the Central African sages of the Ba'ila society observed despondently, "Leza (God) has left us! That is why we experience broken relations, witchcraft, and death."

According to the Ba'ila, Leza is God. Leza means the Besetting One.

"Then we must find Leza and invite him to return among us," exclaimed an old woman.

The old woman was the daughter of tragedy. Her parents died when she was a child. In her older years her relatives, children, even grandchildren had died. She was bereft and lonely.

The leaders of the tribe responded, "You will find Leza at the place where the sky meets the earth."

So the old Ba'ila woman began a safari headed east to find Leza to invite him to return to live among her people.

She passed through the lands of many tribes and chieftainships. Every village she passed asked her, "Where are you going old Ba'ila woman?"

She answered, "East to the place where the sky meets the earth to meet God and invite him to return to live among us."

Day by day she journeyed. On and on she walked and walked, until she died. But she never arrived at the place where sky and earth intercept. She died having never had the chance to meet God.[1]

This story is one of the some 2,000 ancient African myths of creation and separation from God. The African philosopher, John Mbiti, writes,

> It is remarkable that out of these many myths concerning the primeval man and the loss of his original state, there is not a single myth, to my knowledge, which even attempts to suggest a solution or reversal of this great loss.[2]

African Traditional Religions are unanimous in their conviction that the human situation is hopeless; God has left and will never return.

Elusive Hope

African religions are not alone in their conviction that the human situation is hopeless. As I study world religions and philosophies my perception is that themes of hopelessness and meaninglessness run deep in religions and philosophies everywhere.

Do religions give hope?

Several years ago when I was living in Nairobi, Kenya, I took a university class to meet Hindu sages. Their explanation of Vedanta philosophy intrigued us. Vedanta philosophy is based on the ancient Hindu Scriptures known as the Vedas.

Our Hindu teachers told us, "Focus on any god of your choice. Practice meditation that enables you to forget the illusion of individual personhood. Remember that the material world and your sense of being a person is an illusion."

At the end one speaker exclaimed to me, "Life is a tragic accident that should never be. Life is hell. Isn't that true?"

Vedanta Hinduism is not a philosophy of hope; it teaches that my existence is a tragic accident. My goal should be to abandon my illusion of personhood and stop being a person.

In Islam, history has no forward movement. There is no sense of pilgrimage or hope moving us onward toward a future fulfillment. There is no anticipation of movement beyond Adam and Eve. We live in parentheses between creation and the final judgment; paradise will be the reward for those who have God's favor and hell the destiny of those who do not.

Just as is true of African Traditional Religion, Hinduism, or Islam, no religion of humans offers hope of a universal kingdom of peace on earth. The exception is biblical faith wherein God promises a kingdom of peace and righteousness and blessing that will extend "to the ends of the earth" (Zech. 9:10).

Do philosophies give hope?

Like the religions, most often our modern philosophies do not offer hope either. For example, the utopia Marxism promised has seemed more like hell than utopia to millions. That ideology is now largely discredited, thereby contributing to overwhelming malaise in formerly communist societies.

Also, in the liberal democracies of Euro-North America there is a pervasive nihilism. A spirit of meaninglessness prevails. Like the Ba'ila woman, the god of the philosophers is not personally engaged in our human situation. The nineteenth century German philosopher, Friedrich Nietzsche, perceived that in Western culture as a whole the God of biblical faith was dead. He experienced deep depression as he considered the hopelessness provided by the philosophical alternatives.

The Quest that Gives Hope

In dramatic and startling contrast to religions and philosophies of hopelessness, meaninglessness, or a non-movement view of history, biblical faith proclaims "hope!" During the past thirty years, the German theologian Jurgen Moltmann has been noteworthy by inviting the church to rediscover hope as one of the greatest surprises the Christian faith offers.[3]

Hope is the great surprise of the Adam and Eve account described in the last chapter. Their hope came from God, who did not abandon them. While they were hiding in the bushes ashamed of themselves, God came looking for them.

"Where are you?" God called!

"I heard you in the garden, and I was afraid because I was naked; so I hid," they whimpered (Gen. 3:8-10).

God immediately knew what they had done. He knew they had declared their independence. He knew they had decided to turn away from their Creator. God was surely heartbroken. He mourned the loss of a right relationship with the man and woman he had created in his own image, the people with whom he longed for fellowship, conversation, and joyful communion.

God grieves

God grieved for the suffering and death Adam and Eve and their descendants would experience because of their rebellion. He looked deep into the future and knew that in rebellion, humans would bring calamity and death on themselves: there would be broken homes, homeless orphans, crack babies, the rape of Nanking (1937), the holocaust in which seven million Jews would be killed by the Nazis, Hiroshima and Nagasaki would be pulverized by the atomic bomb (1945), there would be torture, genocide, rape, refugees, and some people would eat too much while others starved from lack of food.

God knew that in turning from him, humankind would create such unspeakable tragedies as those in Bosnia, Somalia, Rwanda, Ireland, Lebanon, Palestine, Sudan, Sri Lanka, Kosovo, and Serbia. God grieved profoundly.

God looks for us

Yet God never went away. In fact, God pursued Adam and Eve. They ran from God and hid. Not so God. God ran an interception. He pursued them looking for them until he found them hiding among the bushes. The rest of the Bible is the descriptions of that great pursuit; God looking for us wherever we might be in our garden of life. We might run from God; God also runs, but he runs toward us, never away from us.

Hope for a drug runner

Jesse's story astonished me. We were having lunch together in a Birmingham, Alabama restaurant, as he told me about his life as a drug runner. He had worked with a New York City mob running drugs from Mexico to New York. About a decade ago he had placed $100,000 in a brown bag in the front seat of his car for another drug-purchasing run to Mexico. A few miles down the road he began to cry. He wept so hard he could not drive. He pulled into a side road where he kept crying.

My friend knew God had run an interception on him. He drove up the side road for several hundred yards until he saw a church. He walked into the sanctuary, and in the semi-darkness saw a man at the front kneeling in prayer at the altar. It was the pastor. God had impressed the pastor that there was a man needing help. The pastor was praying that God would bring him into contact with whoever it might be that was ready to make the U-turn toward God.

So the mobster and pastor knelt together in prayer. Indeed God is the great pursuer! God pursues; he also recruits others to work with him in pursuing people, inviting them to turn around and return to their loving Father Creator, God.

In fact, some months after that lunch together, my friend, the former mobster, moved to Mexico to live right in the areas where he once bought drugs. He went as God's ambassador to invite the people he used to work with to spread the death of drug addiction, to make a U-turn toward God the Life-Giver.

Jesus told stories about hope

Jesus told stories to help us appreciate the way God seeks us and pursues us. Jesus described God as a shepherd. Ninety-nine sheep were in the fold when evening came. One sheep was missing that night. We imagine that the night was dangerous with reverberating thunder storms. Wolves might have been prowling. The lost sheep might have fallen into a crevasse among thorns and steep dangerous rocks. Nevertheless, the shepherd went out into the night and looked until he found the lost sheep. He returned late that night filled with joy (Luke 15:1-7). God is like that shepherd; a lost person is like that lost sheep.

Jesus said that a person hiding from God might be compared to a woman's precious coin lost somewhere in her house. (The original Greek tale suggests that this coin was a diamond betrothal ring.) The woman swept her whole house. She looked under every carpet and behind each chair. She cleaned out all her closets. She searched until she found the lost coin. She was delighted when she found her treasure, and invited her friends to a party (Luke 15:8-10).

God is like that woman! A person who has turned away from God is like the lost coin.

Redeeming People

Our rebellion against God runs so deep that much more is needed than an invitation to return home to God. People need to be redeemed from wrong directions and the consequences of declaring independence. We need an inner transformation. We need to be rescued from death and from the hosts under Satan's command. However, the forces of evil will not surrender us easily. Intervention is required. We need redemption.

The Titanic and redemption

There were dramatic redemptions the night the *Titanic*, presumed unsinkable, sank on its maiden voyage when it hit an iceberg in the Atlantic the night of April 14, 1912. The James Cameron film production of *Titanic* cost over $200,000,000, the most ever for a movie. Painstakingly replicated were the early-twentieth-century costumes and decor. I wish, however, that the focus of the film had been on deeper meanings of life and death. The tragedy of the *Titanic* is a parable that reveals our inner soul. Arrogance prevailed as the engineers and captain forced the "unsinkable" ship forward; the steam-driven pistons pounded as the ship raced across the treacherous North Atlantic. Arrogance outweighed caution.

When the iceberg slashed the steel side of the ship, passengers refused to consider the possibility of death. Then as the horrible reality took hold, men with weapons occupied some of the life boats. They left children on board to drown. Even after the ship sank, life boats with ample room stayed away from those in the sea calling for help. The arrogance and selfishness that prevailed that night make this a parable of our world.

There is another theme, however, within the horror, the theme of compassion. Some men refused to enter lifeboats to leave space for women and children. There are accounts of redemptions, where a person would give up life to save another. One such redeemer was a Mennonite missionary from India. Annie Funk was going home to be with her dying mother in Bally, Pennsylvania. A letter received by her mission in India after the ship went down said that Annie gave up her place in a life boat to a mother and child. She gave her life to redeem them.

Redemption is not God's afterthought. Nestled within the Genesis account of the tragedy of Adam and Eve's rebellion is a mysterious promise about redemption. God proclaimed to the serpent, who represents evil, "I will put enmity between you and the woman, and between your offspring and hers; he will crush your head, and you will strike his heel" (Gen. 3:13).

For centuries people of faith were perplexed about the meaning of this intriguing promise that the offspring of the woman would crush the head of the serpent but be wounded in the heel. Even today theologians muse about the meaning of the promise. But many believe, as the late Anabaptist theologian C.K. Leaman did, that this promise is fulfilled in the good news of John 3:16,[4] often called the Golden Text of the Bible. "For God so loved the world that he gave his one and only son, that whoever believes in him shall not perish, but have eternal life."

Later chapters will clarify that John 3:16 refers to Jesus; he entered right into the conflict with Satan and evil in order to redeem us; he was crucified, but has triumphed over evil by crushing the head of the serpent (John 3:15). Christians are often amazed by the unfolding promise and fulfillment in the Biblical narrative. Many Christians do believe the redemption described in John 3:15, 16 fulfills the promise of Genesis 3:15.

The last chapter describes the evil invader who introduced death and rebellion. Our rebellion against God is deep. But in later chapters we explore how the Child (Jesus) born to a woman (Mary) rescues us from evil and death. Our first parents introduced us to sin and death; Jesus redeems us from them.

Education or Redemption

Islam also describes the creation of Adam and Eve. The Muslim Scripture, the Quran, describe Adam and Eve making a mistake. Therefore, God in his mercy sent them guidance. Islam is convinced that all we need is guidance and mercy from God.

This shifts the moral goalposts away from biblical expectations. Muslims are forthright in their assertions that Christian moral ideals are impractical. Muslims remind us that Quranic morality is for the natural man, and readily achievable. Quranic guidance is practical, but the idealism of Jesus is not practical. Since Islamic guidance is suited to our natural inclinations, then, my Muslim friends explain, all that we need is guidance.

Much modern educational theory also assumes that good, need-based instruction is all we need. The American educational philosopher B. F. Skinner believed good people are produced by good environment and education.[5] Good instruction produces good people. That was also a Marxist principle: teach right, organize right, and people will do right.

Shortly before the collapse of the communist system in the USSR, a friend of mine was invited into the Leningrad home of a communist party official. She said, "For seventy years we have tried to create good people through education. We have failed disastrously. What does the Christian faith offer? I have invited you to dinner tonight to talk about that question."

My friend spent the evening sharing the news that God rescues us from sinfulness. Later chapters will explore more of God's intervention to redeem us from the sinfulness and death we experience in turning away from God.

Of course, Christians also believe that truth-based education is important. However, the Christian faith parts ways fundamentally with those religions and philosophies that base their hope for curing the problem of sinfulness through education.

Needed is a more radical solution: redemption from sin. That is what God promised at the beginning, when our sinfulness, like cancer, began its spread through our lives and societies.

The Surprise of Hope

A surprise of the Christian Way is hope. The hope is anchored in the reality that God has not abandoned us. A tragedy of the myth of the Ba'ila woman and the 2,000 other myths across Africa, is that these societies had not heard the astonishing biblical surprise that God has not gone away. Like the Ba'ila woman, many have no awareness that God is here. People have turned away, but God has not turned away from people.

One of my commitments is reading the Bible through every year, beginning to end. Formidable? Not really; it takes only about twenty minutes of reading a day.

Recall that the Old Testament is the portion of the Bible written before Jesus was born. As noted earlier, the books of the Old Testament were written over a thousand- year span. Every year as I read through the roughly 1,500 pages and thirty-nine books of the Old Testament, I am impressed with the focus on hope that provides integration to these narratives.

Sometimes the focus is like a whisper, other times a shout. Yet the focus is always there; live in joyous hope! The Savior is coming! He will intervene! Salvation is assured. He will redeem us! The joyful expectancy of the prophet Isaiah says it well:

> For to us a child is born,
> to us a son is given,
> and the government will be on his shoulders.
> And he will be called
> Wonderful Counselor,
> Mighty God,
> Everlasting Father,
> Prince of Peace.
> Of the increase of his government and peace
> there will be no end. (Isa. 9:6-7)

• • •

God has not abandoned us. What a surprise! We may abandon God but God does not abandon us. When Adam and Eve choose independence from their Creator, God seeks them. Throughout history God keeps seeking. But he not only seeks us, God also enters our lives and history personally to rescue us. That rescue requires redemption!

6

A PEOPLE OF HOPE

Background Scripture: Genesis 12

Our son Jonathan was born in a Christian mission hospital in Jamama, Somalia. Jamama was about 300 miles south of our home in Johar where we were involved in directing a middle school. Grace and our two young daughters flew to Jamama. To save cash, I caught a bus for the day-long trip.

It rained heavily that day. We passengers invested many hours pushing the bus through goo. Late at night we arrived at the Juba River, several miles from Jamama. The bus could not enter the town because of the mud. Most passengers were going on to a farther destination, but one person disembarked who was planning to walk to Jamama, and I asked to join him.

My Somali companion led the way, down the treacherous banks of the river into a wobbly canoe. Crocodiles were motionless as logs along those river banks waiting to surprise their prey. We had no flashlight. It was dark. I was grateful for a guide. After the crossing we started our walk toward Jamama. I fell into the mud not once but several times. It was black cotton soil mud, slippery as smooth wet ice and deep. Frogs were singing a cacophonous choir everywhere and the night closed around us in deep darkness. I could see nothing except the dark shadow of a muddy man sloshing forward just ahead of me.

Then unexpectedly my companion announced, "There it is! See that light! It is the light from the mission hospital."

I was thrilled beyond words. I saw a dim light above the horizon about a mile away. We plodded on through the goo, heading straight toward that beacon set on a high pole. That light filled me with hope and confidence. It guided me to the place where Grace and our two girls, Karen and Doris, were awaiting the birth of Jonathan.

A Light to the Nations

In a similar way, God called a particular people to become a light to the nations. God made a covenant with them; they would be his people and he would be their God. The Lord God declared,

> I will make you a light
> for the Gentiles [nations],
> that you may bring forth my salvation
> to the ends of the earth. (Isa. 49:6)

God invited them to become his covenant people living among the nations. God called them to be a people of hope for the nations. They were to be "a banner for the peoples. . ." (Isa. 11:10).

In earlier chapters we have discovered that God acts in history. What does he do; why does he act? Supremely he acts to form a people who love him, who live in a covenant relationship with him. The drama of biblical history is the astonishing acts of God in calling forth a people who are his people, his witnesses among the nations.

Show and Tell

Children usually enjoy "show and tell" in school. The child takes an object to school and uses it to share something important. I also sometimes do "show and tell" in preaching or teaching.

God's intention was that Israel become his "show and tell." God is a strategic planner; he placed this people in Canaan (present-day Israel/Palestine), at the crossroads of the continents Africa, Asia, and Europe. That was the best location in the whole world for people to notice and meet God's "show and tell."

As noted in Chapter 1, the history of Israel forms the core of the Old Testament Scriptures. There is also ample commentary, teaching, prophecy, and inspirational reflection, which are the writings of prophets or poets. But historical events are the center around which all else revolves.

The historical core of the Bible is a perplexity to people from other faiths who meet these Scriptures for the first time. For example, several years ago, a Muslim friend asked to borrow a Bible from me. The next day he returned it with a look of somber dejection.

"I thought this is Scripture," he lamented. "Alas, it is corrupted, for it is mostly a history book!"

Hindus also consider history as an irrelevancy. The ultimate personal goal of devout Hindus is to become absorbed into the universal soul of the universe. They would experience the Bible to be quite earthly indeed, when compared to the philosophical reflections or moral and ritual instructions that are the centerpiece of Hindu Scripture.

In contrast, Israel was keenly interested in history. In fact, they are the only ancient people who gave serious and sustained attention to writing their history. The Old Testament is, furthermore, the only accurate ancient written history.[1] Israel believed that they were God's appointed "show and tell" people. This is one reason they wanted to record their history accurately.

Embarrassing stories are included

The realism of the accounts is surprising. For example, Abraham, father of the faith-in-God movement, told a lie about his wife, not just once, but twice. He denied that she was his wife because she was so beautiful he thought he might be killed so that a local king could marry her (Gen. 12:10-20; 20).

Furthermore, Abraham, the one called to model the meaning of faith in God, doubted God's Word. God had promised that Abraham's descendants would be numerous like the sand by the sea and the stars in the sky. However, Sarah was past her menses. On one occasion Abraham fell on the ground laughing in disbelief when God promised a son through Sarah; his wife likewise stood behind her tent flaps trying to suppress her chuckles.

So Abraham and Sarah schemed to help God fulfill his promise. Because Abraham did not believe God could bless his aged wife, Sarah, with a child, he slept with Sarah's maid, Hagar (Gen. 16:1-3). The maid bore Abraham a son, Ishmael.

The candor of these stories is amazing. Both the good and the bad are recorded; even the unbelief and lies of Abraham, the father of faith, are included. In most cases when people develop legends about their heroes, they do not include the wrongful or embarrassing things that their heroes did; they tell only of the good. Yet in the Bible both the right and wrong conduct of the heroes is recorded, as is true of the accounts of Abraham and Sarah. The quality of such realism is distinctive of ancient biblical history. God's show and tell does not sweep naughty deeds under the rug.

Skittish about religious ritual

The people of Israel were distinctive in their understanding of history as the arena of God-action meeting human-action. They were not impressed with philosophy, and their prophets were skeptical and critical of religious ritual. They believed that religiosity or philosophical speculation were too often distractions from the real world, a right relationship with the Lord God, and the righteousness that God requires.

Concerning religious ritual, the prophet Isaiah proclaimed,

'The multitude of your sacrifices–
    what are they to me?' says the Lord.
"I have more than enough of burnt offerings,

of rams and the fat of fattened animals;
I have no pleasure
in the blood of bulls and lambs and goats. . . .
Your New Moon festivals and your appointed
feasts my soul hates.
They have become a burden to me;
I am weary of bearing them.
When you spread out your hands in prayer,
I will hide my eyes from you;
even if you offer many prayers,
I will not listen.
Your hands are full of blood;
wash and make yourselves clean.
Take your evil deeds out of my sight!
Stop doing wrong; learn to do right!
Seek justice,
encourage the oppressed.
Defend the cause of the fatherless,
plead the case of the widow." (Isa. 1:11, 14-17)

One of the surprises of the biblical Scriptures is that over the centuries the prophets developed an increasingly intense critique of religious ritual. God required righteousness; the practice of religion should never usurp the commitment to justice!

The futility of philosophy

The book of Ecclesiastes describes the futility of hoping that philosophical speculation will reveal the true meaning of life. The writer concludes,

Of making many books there is no end,
and much study wearies the body.
Now all has been heard;
here is the conclusion of the matter:
Fear God and keep his commandments,
for this is the whole duty of man.
(Eccl. 12:12-13)

It was the acts of God in history that gave Israel hope and purpose, not philosophy or religious ritual. They were captivated by that hope.

Stubborn Hope

The hope that pervades Israel's historical accounts is one of the astonishing distinctions of biblical faith and history. Hope in times of prosperity is understandable, and especially so when Israel prospered as a free nation under great kings such as David and Solomon. However, it is Israel's persistent and stubborn hope in God during adversity that is so amazing.

This is especially true in the sixth century B.C. when Israel was attacked by powerful armies from Egypt in the south and Babylon in the north. Finally Jerusalem was utterly destroyed by the Babylonian army. Its magnificent temple was burned, the precious treasures stolen, and the walls flattened. The battle for Jerusalem involved unspeakable atrocities and famine. Most of those who survived the slaughter were taken into captivity to far away Babylon; others fled to Egypt. This era of captivity is known as the exile.

Throughout those horrible times, prophets proclaimed that God was judging Israel for her sins. They also proclaimed the promise that God would never abandon his people. Prophets such as Isaiah proclaimed that even in their suffering, Israel was a light to the nations. Hope prevailed against all odds.

The prophet Jeremiah is typical of this surprising and stubborn hope. He lived through the horrendous suffering when the Babylonians destroyed Jerusalem.

Jeremiah wrote,

> I remember my affliction and my wandering,
>   the bitterness and the gall.
> I will remember them,
>   and my soul is downcast in me.
> Yet this I call to mind

and therefore I have hope:
Because of the Lord's great love
    we are not consumed,
    for his compassions never fail.
They are new every morning;
    great is your faithfulness.
    I say to myself, "The Lord is my portion;
    therefore I will wait for him."
The Lord is good to those whose hope is in him,
    to the one who seeks him;
it is good to wait quietly
    for the salvation of the Lord. (Lam. 3:19-26)

Israel's hope in the calamity of the exile was rooted in their memory of God's astonishing acts in their earlier history. We will explore several of these amazing events.

Unforgettable Surprises

The story of Israel was formed by unforgettable surprises. These were root events that significantly formed the hope themes in Israel's history. As mentioned in chapter 1, the Jewish theologian, Emil Fackenheim, writes of Israel's "root experiences" that nurtured an "abiding astonishment."[2] These surprising root experiences were Israel's abiding "show and tell." They nurtured unquenchable hope.

We will explore five of these hope-creating surprises.

A first surprise is God's call to Abraham (Gen. 12:1-9). Abraham and Sarah lived in Mesopotamia, in the region of present-day Iraq. Doubtless they enjoyed a good life living in the fertile upper reaches of the Tigris and Euphrates Rivers. The Mesopotamians worshiped nature divinities; a favorite was the moon which they named Sin.

What happened is totally astounding. God who created the moon and all other phenomena on earth and in the heavens called to Abraham, saying,

> "Leave your country, your people and your father's
>   household and go to the land I will show you.
> I will make you into a great nation
>   and I will bless you;
> I will make your name great
>   and you will be a blessing.
> I will bless those who bless you,
>   and whoever curses you I will curse;
> and all the peoples on earth
>   will be blessed through you." (Gen. 12:1-3)

God promised to bless Abraham and make him to be a blessing to all peoples on the earth.

"You will be the father of many nations," God promised extravagantly. "I will establish my covenant as an everlasting covenant between me and you and your descendants after you for the generations to come, to be your God and the God of your descendants after you" (Gen. 17:4,7).

This event just over 4,000 years ago is one of the most astounding spiritual and cultural watersheds in all of human history. Today more than three billion people on Earth profess to be the heirs of the faith of Abraham: Jews, Christians, and Muslims. Abraham's descendants are not only those who trace their genealogy to him; tribes and nations around the world consider Abraham to be their father in faith.

Before Abraham and Sarah, people everywhere believed that nature and divinity participated in oneness. With very rare exceptions, indeed, the worship of expressions of nature was universal. That view of nature began with Adam and Eve; recall that they turned to a tree for their authority rather than to God the creator of the tree.

I have referred to this understanding of nature as ontocratic. We have alluded to the Babylonian Tiamat myth as an example of the notion that nature is a god or gods. The ancient Babylonians of Mesopotamia believed the earth came about in battle between the gods Marduk and the mother of all gods,

Tiamat. Marduk slew Tiamat; the earth and the heavens were the carcass of the dead god Tiamat. Belief in such gods of nature was pervasive.

These myths kept changing, and we are unsure at what stage of development the myths were at the time of Abraham; written documents come to us several centuries after Abraham. Nevertheless, Abraham was called to break with the gods of nature.

"Leave!" God commanded.

In saying yes to God's call, Abraham and Sarah were breaking with the religious assumptions of all other surrounding peoples, and becoming the pioneers of a faith movement that now includes people from every region of the earth. They became the parents of the beginnings of a movement that broke with all ontocratic religion. God is not nature. God is other than creation. God is the righteous personal one who calls us, and invites us into a covenant relationship with him.

Take note; the turning away from nature divinities did not happen without conflict. God formed a covenant with Abraham and his descendants; Israel was their name. For at least the next fifteen hundred years these covenant people were in conflict with the nature gods. Yet they found the fertility gods of nature enticing. Repeatedly they forsook their creator and returned to the nature gods of fertility; trees and green hills were especially seductive. Yet God persisted. For centuries he kept pounding into their heads that only God the creator is God. None other!

God's promise to Abraham also turned all other ancient assumptions about blessing upside down. The assumption of all other peoples was that the blessing of divinity empowers one to subjugate others, not bless them.

All the Babylonian myths about the gods of nature were violent. Might makes right was the rule of the gods. Humanity came forth through violent conflict among the gods. Of course, society was expected to do just as the gods did, the powerful subjugating the weak.[3]

However, God's promise to Abraham introduced an astonishing new understanding of the nature of God's blessing on his people. God blesses his people expecting that they will be a blessing to their neighbors and to all nations. He called Abraham away from any notion that might makes right. Abraham was called to abandon socio-religious violence. He was to bless people, not to kill them.

God also promised the land of Canaan to Abraham and his descendants. However, the way in which God provided the land was through Abraham's conduct as a good neighbor. In fact, when Sarah died, Abraham paid an exorbitant price to the local Hittites for a field in which to bury her. Abraham never fought for land. It was God who provided land as Abraham gained the favor of the Canaanites among whom he lived.

A second surprise is so unusual that it makes us chuckle; this is the birth of Isaac (Gen. 21:1-21). God made a covenant with Abraham. He promised that his wife, Sarah, would bear a son. God's covenant of blessing for the nations through all generations would rest on that son and his descendants. God promised to bless Ishmael born to Hagar, also, but the son of the covenant promise would be born to ninety-year-old Sarah.

Both Abraham and Sarah struggled as they tried to believe this impossible promise. Sarah was too old! Both Abraham and Sarah laughed at God's ridiculous promise; they just knew Sarah could not have a baby. Nevertheless, God fulfilled his promise. Isaac was born to Sarah. Isaac means laughter, for Sarah observed wryly that people will laugh when they hear that a ninety-year-old woman had a baby.

This root experience reveals that hope is a gift from God. We do not carry responsibility to fulfill God's promises. That is God's responsibility. A people of hope are called to trust and obey God. He gives his people surprises of joy and laughter as he fulfills his promises.

A third surprising root event is the exodus from Egypt (Exod. 3-14). In the course of time the descendants of Abraham, Isaac, and his son Jacob moved to Egypt to escape famine in Palestine. They multiplied in Egypt and in four hundred years they had become a nation approaching two million people. They were enslaved by Pharaoh, the ruler of Egypt, and forced into hard labor.

God intervened in this calamity. Moses was God's spokesperson in the confrontation with Pharaoh. God sent ten plagues on the land of Egypt to persuade Pharaoh to release the People of Israel: the water turned to blood, frogs were everywhere, as were gnats and flies, livestock died, boils appeared, and hail, locusts, and darkness occurred. Nevertheless Pharaoh resisted. He needed the slave labor of the Israeli people.

Finally one night God sent the angel of death, and the first born in homes throughout the land died. The people of Israel were excepted, however, as were all others who had daubed the blood of a slain lamb on their door lintels and posts in accordance with God's command. God passed over those homes which had the blood of the lamb at the entranceway.

That event is the origin of the Jewish Passover Feast. The Passover festival is a reminder of the night the angel of death passed over the homes marked by the blood of a slain lamb.

(The blood of the slain lamb sprinkled on the door-posts and lintels is a sign pointing toward a universal truth. In Chapter 8 we will explore that truth.)

On that Passover night, Pharaoh and Egypt freed Israel and sent them out of the land. They headed toward the northern shores and marshes of the Red Sea. God sent a strong east wind that pushed the waters aside, and they crossed the sea in safety.

When Pharaoh changed his mind about releasing Israel from enslavement, he pursued them into the Red Sea. His chariots became stuck in the sand. When the sea waters returned to their place, Pharaoh and his army were drowned.

This deliverance from slavery is one of the most significant root experiences of biblical faith. Throughout the biblical Scriptures, this exodus from slavery has nurtured praise and amazement. The exodus, as no other event, formed Israel into a people of hope. God intervened in an astonishing manner to deliver them from slavery.

There is, therefore, hope for oppressed peoples. In modern times liberation movements for the oppressed around the world have been encouraged by this biblical event.

Repeatedly in the confrontation with Pharaoh, Moses commanded the Egyptian ruler, in the name of the Lord, "Let my people go" (Exod. 5:1; 7:16; 8:1, 20; 9:1, 13; 10:3). That expression of faith, hope, confidence, and command has encouraged and empowered liberation movements as diverse as the 1950s civil rights struggle in the United States, or the conflict with the apartheid regime in South Africa before the 1994 democratic elections.

In other contexts even Marxist revolutionaries such as Mao Tse-Tung in China or Che Guevara in Latin America have been inspired by the exodus in struggles for liberation from exploitative political and economic systems. Although the exodus might encourage a Marxist struggle, there are significant differences between Marxist ideology and the biblical event.

It is noteworthy that God intervened to bring about the exodus; in Marxism the liberation struggle is only a human endeavor. In the biblical account, God intended that Israel struggle nonviolently; in Marxism, violent revolution is essential. In the biblical account, trust in God empowered Israel to confront Pharaoh nonviolently. In Marxist atheism, there is no God to trust; violence is, therefore, mandatory.

Know this! God does hear the prayers of the oppressed.

A fourth transforming event is the covenant at Mount Sinai (Exod. 19-20). After the exodus, the Israelites began a slow trek north through the deserts toward Canaan, the land God had promised for the descendants of Abraham. They encamped at Mount Sinai, which is about half way across the desert from Egypt to the land of Canaan where Abraham, Isaac, and Jacob with their families had once lived.

God met this motley throng at the desert Mount. God's presence on the mountain was tremendous. His presence was accompanied with thunder, lightening, and trumpet. The people were in fear. They knew they were encountering God, their righteous creator. They put a fence around the mountain so that no one would presumptuously get too close to the presence of God on that mountain.

God made a covenant with them at that mountain. The Ten Commandments formed the covenant's spiritual and ethical core. In short, these covenant commandments said: no other gods, no idols, no profanity, rest on the Sabbath, honor parents, no killing of humans, no adultery, no theft, no false testimony, no covetousness (Exod. 20:1-17). God's covenant with these several hundred thousand campers in the Mount Sinai desert was an invitation to become a people of hope and righteousness.

At the Mount, God instructed Moses on the construction of the place of worship that became the tabernacle (Exod. 25–31). For many years this collapsible tent was their worship center. The Ark of the Covenant was a small gold-plated acacia box kept in the tabernacle in a little room called the Holy of Holies.

Various objects were kept in the Ark, but probably the most significant was the Ten Commandments engraved on two stone tablets. There was a mercy seat on the lid covering the Ark. This mercy seat covering the Ten Commandments was a sign that people met both God's law and mercy as they worshiped him.

After the tabernacle was completed and dedicated for the worship of God, the people observed the signs of God's presence above and in the tabernacle. A pillar of cloud hovered above the tabernacle in the day time, and at night the pillar was seen as fire. God's glory also filled the Holy of Holies, where the Ark was kept. A thick curtain partitioned the Holy of Holies from the other areas of the tabernacle.

The tabernacle was a tent, easily moved. Whenever the pillar of cloud or fire rose from above the tabernacle, the people collapsed their tents and prepared for journey. They traveled through the desert following the cloudy or fiery pillar. This was God's way of leading them forward. As a people of hope, they were a people on the move. Hope looks forward in expectancy! Hope moves us onward.

God's plan was that Israel extend the gift of hope to all peoples. For this reason Israel was for many centuries a remarkably open community. Others were welcome to join with Israel in the pilgrimage of hope. Although families in Israel respected and traced genealogical descent from Abraham, the covenant community was open to all others who wished to become part of this people of hope. Even in the exodus from Egypt, they were a mixed multitude (Exod. 12:38).

King David, whose life is described in the next section, is an example of the open nature of Israel to people who were not direct descendants of Abraham. His companions were both from Israel and an array of surrounding nationalities. There is literate opinion that King David might himself have had personal family ties with the Ammonites.[4] The listings of leaders and genealogies in Israel are salted with names of people from outside the ethnic bonding of genealogical descent from Abraham.

The entire Old Testament, written over a 1,000-year span, is an account of Israel's unfolding understanding of what it meant to be a people of hope and blessing among the nations. Throughout the centuries their experience has significantly influenced many societies: rest from your work one day in seven, respect the freedom and dignity of the person, the person is infinitely more valuable than property, forgive the debtors rather than throw them into jail, care for the refugees and the poor, care for the good earth. Kings and governors do not have ultimate authority. They also stand under the demands of justice.

We could add more. Suffice it to say that the core values of the United Nations' Universal Declaration of Human Rights are indebted to the Old Testament accounts of Israel as a people called to be God's "show and tell" of hope among the nations.

For 3,500 years Israel has never forgotten the abiding astonishment of the Mount Sinai covenant-making event. The first five books of the Bible, known as the Torah, are Scriptures that developed in response to that root event. Today those Scriptures are at the soul of every Sabbath worship in Jewish synagogues around the world.

A fifth, almost hilarious surprise, was God's promise to King David (1 Samuel 19:1-20:21). First, a bit of background history. For forty years after the exodus from Egypt, the people of Israel lived as animal-herding nomads in the deserts south and east of Canaan. Then they began to occupy the land of Canaan that God had promised to Abraham. In contrast to Abraham's story, this occupation was often violent, as they defeated the local inhabitants in battle.

These wars require significant theological reflection, an exploration that is beyond the scope of this book. Although peace is God's intention for all nations, the Old Testament writers describe God's intervention in these wars. God usually intervened on behalf of Israel, sometimes in most dramatic ways. However, God also used defeat on the battlefield to chasten Israel and to turn their hearts away from an attitude of arrogance so that they might repent and return to God. The Old Testament views Israel's victory over the Canaanites as one way in which God expressed his judgment upon the wickedness of these nations (Deut. 7).

After some centuries of settling into Canaan, Israel decided they wanted a king. Saul was the first king. He was not a righteous man. After a tumultuous reign, David became king, but not without several years of struggle and inter-clan skirmishes.

King David had moral blemishes, including a catastrophic slip into adultery with Bathsheba and the arranged death of her husband Uriah. Yet David returned to God in contrition and repentance. Whenever he sinned, he made the U-turn to God. When he received rebuke for his sinfulness, he repented; he was called a man after God's own heart... (1 Sam. 13:14).

During his reign David observed that the ark of God was still kept in a tent, six centuries after the encounter with God at Mount Sinai. He decided that the Ark needed a temple. David spoke with his advisers about the idea, and they thought it was excellent.

However, the Prophet Nathan came to David with counsel from God. God did not need a house for the Ark of the Covenant. The tent that moves from place to place was better suited to the worship of a people of hope and pilgrimage. Furthermore, David had fought in many wars. If the people wished to build a temple, then David's son, who would reign after him, should build that temple, but not David whose hands had killed many people (1 Chron. 22:8).

This is not to suggest that God did not intervene to give David victory over his enemies. The Scriptures indicate that God did intervene (2 Sam. 7:9), for David's heart was ultimately turned toward God. Yet God's highest will for all humankind is peace (Zech. 9:10). God made it clear that the person who would build his temple should be a man of peace.

It was keenly disappointing to David that he could not build the temple. But then came an astounding promise. The prophet Nathan continued with the message from God, "Your house and your kingdom will endure forever before me; your throne will be established forever" (2 Sam. 17:16). Instead of David building a house for God, God had promised to establish David's house forever, meaning his kingly line. David was overwhelmed. He went to the place of prayer and sat before the Lord in astonishment.

David prayed,

> Who am I, O Sovereign Lord, and what is my family, that you have brought me this far? And as if this were not enough in your sight, O Sovereign Lord, you have also promised you, so that your name will be great forever. (2 Sam. 7:18, 19, 25, 26)

Neither King David nor Israel ever lost their amazement at that promise. The biblical prophets picked up on this theme with a consistency that is astonishing: a king will come who will reign on David's throne forever. They held on to this hope amid calamitous adversity.

Within six centuries of David's reign, most of the Israelis were dispersed as refugees among strange nations. They had no king. Yet the confident hope persisted; God will appoint a son of David to establish David's kingship forever.

Surprises of Grace and Peace

God intended that Israel be a beacon of hope among the nations. We have described only five transforming surprises that helped to form Israel into a people of hope. Their story includes much more, but the events described above were not an interesting side show. They were, in Fackenheim's words, "root experiences" that created an "abiding astonishment."

The riddle of peace and violence

As mentioned above, one of the perplexities of Israel as a people of hope is the violent manner in which they occupied Canaan. That conquest continued intermittently for some centuries. After they settled in Canaan and became a political state, they were sometimes embroiled in colossal wars with neighboring nations. Sometimes they fought civil wars against one another.

Yet they were called by God to be a people of hope and blessing to the nations. Nevertheless, God also made it clear that those who reject the people who extend the blessings of God, those rejecters will be cursed (Gen. 12:1-3). God is the Life Giver; when we reject the Life Giver, the consequence is death.

It is intriguing that in each of the five root events we have described above, the people of the covenant were invited to trust and obey God rather than use human scheming to bring about God's blessing. The stories describing Abraham and Moses encourage avoiding violence. The story about King David that we have explored does not criticize David for his violence in warfare, but it does raise concerns about David's warrior history.[5] I will review the subtle critique of violence nurtured in the soul of each of these stories: Abraham, Moses, and David.

1. God provided a place for Abraham in Canaan through Abraham being a good neighbor, not through his military conquest. In other Scriptures that we have not referred to, we discover that the same stance was embraced by Abraham's son, Isaac, and his grandson, Jacob (Gen. 26:12-33; 34:1-35:15).

2. Moses led Israel from Egypt, not with violent revolution, but through God's intervention. God, not Moses, took vengeance against those who oppressed Israel.

3. King David was prohibited from building a temple because he was a man of war.

Thus, although violence was a significant theme throughout Israel's history, it is noteworthy that a number of the most significant core experiences in the formation of Israel held forth an alternative vision. It was a vision of a people of peace and hope, who trusted God for justice and their defense. They were to be a light to the nations showing the way to God.

God's plan was that Israel would "show and tell" the nations of his love for all peoples; however, God is also very clear that those who reject his love will experience his judgment. The Israelites were to invite the nations to repent their evil and turn to God.

Jonah, the Rebellious Missionary

This meant that Israel was to be a missionary people-nation, showing and telling all nations about God and his love. A tiny book in the Old Testament, Jonah, describes the plight of one missionary from Israel, named Jonah (c. eighth century B.C.). God had commissioned Jonah to go to Nineveh as a missionary.

That was Jonah's nightmare. Jonah was not impressed with God's compassionate concern for all nations, and especially Nineveh, which Jonah hated. He wanted Israel to enjoy the blessings of God, but he didn't want other nations to enjoy those blessings; and especially not the enemies of Israel. He wanted the destruction, not the salvation, of Israel's enemies.

Nevertheless, God called Jonah to be a missionary to Nineveh, a great city to the north of Israel that was one of Israel's most feared enemies. God commanded Jonah to preach in Nineveh that God was going to destroy this wicked city.

Jonah refused! He boarded a ship and sailed in the opposite direction toward Tarshish. A storm struck. The sailors threw Jonah overboard because he told them the storm must be God's judgment on his disobedience. God sent a large fish to swallow him. Apparently finding the missionary indigestible, the fish vomited Jonah onto the land.

In contrition, Jonah went to Nineveh to preach. However, he was horrified when the inhabitants of Nineveh repented of their sins, and turned to God. God declared that Nineveh was forgiven for its sins, and the destruction of Nineveh would not happen.

Missionary Jonah was furious. In an astonishing classic of all missionary literature, Jonah angrily accused God:

> O Lord, is this not what I said when I was still at home. That is why I was so quick to flee to Tarshish. I knew that you are a gracious and compassionate God, slow to anger and abounding in love, a God who relents from sending calamity. Now, O Lord, take away my life, for it is better for me to die than to live. (Jon. 4:2-3)

God's Surprise for the Nations

Missionary Jonah's vision for the nations was utterly opposite from God's vision, and his vision was also vastly different than that of the prophet Isaiah, who was probably Jonah's contemporary. Isaiah was thrilled with a vision of God extending salvation and peace to all nations. He writes,

> They will neither harm nor destroy
> on all my holy mountain,
> for the earth will be full of the
> knowledge of the Lord
> as the waters cover the sea.
> In that day the Root of Jesse (David's Son)
> will stand as a banner for the peoples;
> the nations will rally to him,
> and his place of rest will be glorious.
> (Isa. 11:9-10)

• • •

Five transforming surprises—that is what we have explored in this chapter: 1) God's call to Abraham, 2) the birth of Isaac, 3) the exodus from Egypt, 4) the covenant at Sinai, and 5) God's promise to David. The terrific suffering and disappointment of the exile was also exceedingly significant. The abiding astonishment of these surprises formed Israel, and continues to shape the mission of both Israel and the church in our modern times. Without these central surprises of biblical faith, there would be no Israel or church. There would be no Bible either.

Jonah's mission to Nineveh and what happened there shows that God is indeed the God of surprises! Jonah wished that God would not surprise us with his grace and mercy; that is why Jonah went into a terrible funk, a depression, and wished he could die. He wanted God to burn the city of Nineveh, not have mercy on it. He did not want the world beyond little Israel to be touched with the surprises of God's love and mercy.

But God saw things differently. He delights in surprising every one of us!

7

IMMANUEL

Background Scripture: Luke 1:26-2:20

"It seems like a lot of wasted space in the universe, if there is no one else out there," muses radioastronomer Eleanor Arroway in the Robert Zemeckis film, *Contact*. She and a consortium of agencies and foundations invested millions of dollars developing listening technologies to hear possible messages from beings in outer space. When they thought they had received a signal from intelligent life from the region of the star Vega, the whole world was caught up in exhilaration and anticipation.

The Vegans had sent instructions on how to build a machine to visit them. Governments invested a trillion dollars developing these machines. Alas the machines blew up. Subsequent investigation indicated the signals were probably a farce. However, Eleanor continued to believe against all odds that she had made contact with life on Vega.

One of Eleanor's friends was a technician working in economic development in poor nations. He believed in God. He assured her that he had also experienced communication from out there. It was communication from God. She was incredulous, preferring her technological approach to searching for messages from out there.

This film, based on a Carl Sagan science fiction novel, reveals the yearning of people for communication from someone out there. Without that communication, we on planet earth are lonely. Our expectation is that people would celebrate joyfully to be in communication with someone out there who is concerned for us.

In Chapter 4 I suggested that an invasion from "out there" has already occurred. It happened at the beginning of human history when the battle between good and evil came into the first human family.

However, God has not abandoned us. A new Adam would be born to woman; he would assure the triumph of good over evil, of life over death. The Son is Immanuel, meaning God with us.

Salvation for the Nations

This chapter introduces the arrival and ministry of the new Adam, the promised Savior. He has come. He is the promised "guest" sent from God. He is Immanuel, God with us. His name is Jesus Christ.

There is no hiding behind bushes in fear and shame like Adam and Eve did. Instead, for those who receive him, there is dancing in the streets. The Savior has come! He offers salvation and blessing among the nations.

I have observed that salvation in the most varied and interesting places, such as in the highlands of Guatemala. The Alta Verapaz night was thick with darkness. We trod a mile sloshing through mud towards the church in Pocola'. The night was cold, rainy, and foggy in the Ke'chi'-inhabited highlands of Guatemala.

At the Pocola' Church we were ushered to the front. Our bench was a backless plank. The floor was damp and earthen. Some of the assembling worshipers had walked many miles through mud and rain that evening. Most had no shoes.

As worshipers arrived, they went forward and knelt in prayer at the worn wooden rail in front of the pulpit. I had a front row view of their feet. I saw the soles of thick, cracked, muddy, bare feet. They were the feet of children, mothers, fathers, singles, married, and grandparents kneeling in prayer. These were feet that had walked across mountains and valleys, through cold rain and muddy goo, to gather with others in worship that night. They were the feet of the poor.

I thought of the Prophet Isaiah who once exclaimed,

How beautiful on the mountains

are the feet of those who bring good news... (Isa. 52:7).

They kept coming, one after another, beautiful feet. When one pair left to find a seat, another pair would take their place.

When the singing began, I wept with joy.

The combination of beautiful feet of praying people in front of me and joyful songs behind me was overwhelming. I turned from admiring feet to looking into the faces singing in the audience: old and crinkled faces, young and soft faces. All were singing with total exuberant joy.

"What joyous singing!" I exclaimed to Dennis Witmer, my translator.

He responded, "In the traditional Ke'chi' culture there is no singing. Perhaps the oppression and tragedy they have suffered from those who have taken over their traditional homelands has robbed them of song. However, when they meet Jesus, a song comes into their souls."

"When a Ke'chi' is baptized, she prays, 'God, please, teach me to sing!'"

We had a party that evening. Recall that God had promised Abraham 4,000 years ago that he would be the father of nations. That night in the highlands of Alta Verapaz we joined one of those nations in joyful worship and celebration for the faithfulness of the God of Abraham, who was now also their God.

The Savior Has Come

In the previous two chapters we have explored God's promises to Abraham and Sarah, to Israel, and to King David. Those chapters only surveyed some ways that God gave hope.

Now we begin an exploration of the New Testament; the Old Testament are the biblical Scriptures written before the birth of Jesus, who is the promised Savior. The New Testament describes his life, teaching and ministry (the four gospels: Matthew, Mark, Luke, and John), a history of the early church (Acts), and letters concerning Christian theology and teaching (the epistles).

The New Testament announces with clarity that the arrival of the promised Savior inaugurates the kingdom of God on earth; hope and joy characterize this kingdom. One of C. S. Lewis's early books, *Surprised by Joy*, tells of the transforming joy of meeting the Savior.[1] Recently Tony Campolo has developed the same theme in *The Kingdom of God is a Party*.[2] In this chapter we explore the joy we experience as we welcome Jesus the Savior, the Guest whom God has sent into our world.

Two of the gospel writers, Luke and Matthew, describe the birth of Jesus. Luke's report of intimate details points to the possibility that he or his sources may have had the opportunity to have a personal conversation with Mary, the mother of Jesus.

Mary is surprised

Luke reports that God sent an angel by the name of Gabriel to a virgin called Mary who lived in Nazareth.

Mary was startled and astonished when the angel greeted and told her,

> Do not be afraid, Mary, you have found favor with God. You will be with child and give birth to a son, and you are to give him the name Jesus. He will be great and will be called the Son of the Most High. The Lord God will give him the throne of . . . David, and he will reign over the house of Jacob forever; his kingdom will never end. . . . The Holy Spirit will come on you, and the power of the Most High will overshadow you. So the holy one to be born will be called the Son of God. (Luke 1:30-33, 35)

Although Mary was a virgin and engaged for marriage to Joseph, she replied, "I am the Lord's servant. . . . May it be to me as you have said" (Luke 1:38).

In a small town like Nazareth 2,000 years ago, an out of wedlock pregnancy was a scandal. For an engaged girl it could mean death by stoning. This pregnancy was not a tidy affair. Matthew reports that until an angel of the Lord counseled otherwise, Joseph considered breaking the engagement. Joseph had not fathered this child. No man was involved in this conception. Mary was a virgin. The conception of Jesus Christ in Mary was a miracle wrought through the power of the Spirit of God.

Mary visits Elizabeth

Mary's family and friends could not comprehend what had happened. Escaping the town's dismay and gossip, Mary left Nazareth for the village where her cousin Elizabeth lived. Elizabeth was also pregnant; her son was destined to become John the Baptist, whose ministry was to prepare Israel for the mission of Jesus.

As Mary came into Elizabeth's home, she sang a song of overflowing joy. We note several lines in this joyous song,

> My soul glorifies the Lord,
>   and my spirit rejoices in God my Savior . . .
> He has filled the hungry with good things
>   but has sent the rich away empty.
> He has helped his servant Israel,
>   remembering to be merciful
> to Abraham and his descendants forever,
>   even as he said to our fathers.
> (Luke 1:46-47,53-55)

Outsiders Welcome Jesus

The same theme of joy, even in adversity, cascades on Bethlehem in Judea where Jesus was born. Joseph had taken heavily pregnant Mary on the hundred mile journey from their hometown of Nazareth, south to Bethlehem to be registered in a Roman census. The inn was full; they slept in a cattle stall. That night Jesus was born.

Luke describes a joyous choir filling the heavens. A company of angels appeared to shepherds on the outskirts of Bethlehem singing,

> Glory to God in the highest,
> and on earth peace to men on
> whom his favor rests. (Luke 2:14)

Shepherds were outsiders of Jewish society. Yet they slipped into Bethlehem and saw and worshiped the newborn whose bed was a manger.

In Matthew's account, far away in eastern lands, wise men saw a special star. They followed that star to Bethlehem, and gave the child gifts fit for a king: gold, frankincense, and myrrh.

The shepherds were on the outside edges of society, much like the Ke'chi' of Alta Verapaz are on the outer edges of Guatemalan society. The wise men were in all likelihood Gentiles (non Jewish people) from nations for whom Israel had little respect. It was these shepherds and wise men who came to worship Jesus; those whom one would expect to have welcomed the King didn't even notice that he had been born.

There was an exception; King Herod learned of Jesus' birth from the wise men. Evil Herod had killed his own wife and several sons whom he suspected of plotting against him. When he heard from the eastern wise men that a king had been born in Bethlehem, he ordered all boy babies in the village to be slaughtered. He hoped to kill Jesus along with the other infants.

An angel warned Joseph of the murderous danger. The family escaped as refugees to a strange land, Egypt. Jesus' early childhood was in Africa, far from Israel. Strangely, that is the nature of Jesus, and the celebration he invites us to enjoy. Those you would expect to be present and supportive, such as religious people or the well-to-do are often absent. Those you least expect, such as outcasts and foreigners, are at the center of the dance enjoying it all.

After things quieted down back home in Israel and King Herod had died, Joseph and Mary returned to Nazareth with Jesus. He might have worked with Joseph as a carpenter. When he was about thirty years old, he began his public ministry. Three years later, he was crucified. But that did not end his ministry, as we shall see in the following chapters.

Wine for a Wedding

About the time Jesus began his public ministry, he went to a wedding in Cana with a group of his companions. They ran out of wine, perhaps because Jesus had brought so many friends along to the wedding. His mother told him about the embarrassing situation. Jesus rebuked his mother gently. He seemed concerned that solving the wine problem miraculously would create unwholesome and distracting curiosity concerning Jesus.

Yet Jesus sympathized with the embarrassment the wine crisis created for his mother and the other hostesses. Jesus told the servants to fill six stone jars with water, twenty to thirty gallons in each. Then he told them to take some from the jars and give it to the host. It was excellent wine, better than the wine at the beginning of the wedding (John 2:1-10).

This was the first of his "miraculous signs" (John 2:11). A wedding is one of the most joyous events in human experience. Weddings are characterized in societies everywhere as the time for a real celebration. In this miracle, Jesus was making a statement. Come and enjoy the celebration! All life's parties become better when Jesus is there and in charge.

Miracles are Windows

All of Jesus' miracles are windows into the abundant life and joy God invites us to enjoy.

Jesus was conservative in performing miracles. He did not seek sensationalism, although his miracles did sometimes create a tremendous furor. He preferred to use something at hand in performing the miracle. At the wedding, he did not just wave his hands, and presto, there was wine in every goblet. First, the servants filled huge stone jars with about 150 gallons of water. They worked hard.

Jesus' miracles often required the faith and cooperation of other people. When Jesus fed 5,000 men plus women and children, he used the gift of a lunch from a little boy, five loaves and two fishes. He used an inadequate amount of food and turned it into a blessing for everyone. The people cooperated by sitting in groups. Jesus broke the bread and fish; his disciples distributed it in an orderly manner (Matt. 14:13-21; Mark 6:32-44; Luke 9:10-17; John 6:1-13).

Jesus worked in cooperation with the gifts of creation already present. He expected the cooperation of others. He served in dependency on God in all his miracle-working ministry. Every miracle was ministry related, enabling people to experience wholeness and new life.

Yet his miracles did not open the eyes of all the blind people living in Israel. Neither were all the dead raised to life, nor all the deaf able to hear, nor all the lame free to walk. All who came to him for healing were healed, but not all could come. Why did he not heal everyone just by speaking the word?[3]

It is important to recognize that miracles are windows into the future when Jesus and his kingdom will be established forever. Christians believe that when the kingdom of God is fulfilled, there will be a bodily resurrection of the dead (see more discussion in chapter 10). If all ill people were healed, there would be no need for the resurrection of the dead in the future; we would live forever now without a resurrection. Only at the resurrection of the dead at the concluding drama of history will we experience the total and permanent healing of the total body.

Miracles are signs of the wholeness and new life that we shall someday enjoy fully. They are windows into a future where all sin and evil and suffering will be banished forever. They reveal that God will not bring in his kingdom alone; he needs our cooperation and participation.

A German theologian, Jurgen Moltmann, comments, "Jesus' healings are not supernatural miracles in a natural world. They are the only truly 'natural' things in a world that is unnatural, demonized and wounded."[4] Miracles are God's amen to his promise, that the reign of the eternal King has already begun and will be fully consummated in the future.

Jesus Takes Charge

People were filled with joy and glorified God for the miracles of Jesus. Yet not all did so, because Jesus said and did preposterous things. "No one ever spoke the way this man does," exclaimed the police on one occasion as they tried to explain the reason they had disobeyed an order to arrest Jesus (John 7:46).

Take note of some of the arenas wherein Jesus disturbed the status quo.

Religion

On more than one occasion Jesus enraged religious authorities by healing a person on the Sabbath day, the day when no Jew was permitted to work. They stubbornly insisted that Jesus was terribly wrong to give sight to a blind man (John 9) or cure a man's warped and twisted hand (Mark 3:1-6) on the Sabbath day. This made Jesus deeply angry. He ruthlessly confronted those who practiced religious piety without compassion. Jesus exclaimed, "You are whitewashed tombs, which look beautiful on the outside but on the inside are full of dead men's bones and everything unclean" (Matt. 23:27).

In one icy confrontation the religious leaders were appalled when Jesus declared, "You belong to your father, the devil, and you want to carry out your father's desire" (John 8:44).

Relations and attitudes

Jesus not only healed on the Sabbath; he scandalized and perplexed the multitudes by claiming to be greater than Abraham or greater even than King David himself (John 8:58, Luke 20:41-44). Jesus taught with just that kind of authority. For example, in Jesus' much celebrated Sermon on the Mount (Matt. 5-7) "the crowds were amazed at his teaching, because he taught as one who had authority, and not as their teachers of the law" (7:28-29).

Jesus zeroed in on the core issues of inner thoughts and attitudes. He had come to fulfill the teachings and hopes of the former prophets by revealing the true meaning of their teaching. He highlighted a number of the key laws from the Torah of the Prophet Moses, including the Ten Commandments.

Then he added, "But I tell you . . . "

What did Jesus tell them? Here are several examples of his astonishing teaching.

Deal with the root causes of murder by turning away from the anger and broken relations that produce murder.

Avoid adultery by having pure eyes and a pure heart.

Do not break the one flesh union of marriage through divorce and remarriage; Moses permitted divorce because people's hearts were hard, but that was not in God's plan for a husband and wife.

Never swear oaths; rather be a person of truth, always.

The principle of an eye for an eye that Moses taught is not consistent with a commitment to serving and loving the one who has done you wrong. Practice love for your enemy, not hate.

Do not seek material wealth; give generously. Trust God and do not worry about anything.

Good news ethics

The ethics Jesus taught are good news. In fact, Jesus concluded the Sermon on the Mount by saying that anyone who does not obey these ethical teachings is building his house on sand. When the storm comes, his house will collapse. However, the person who practices the teachings of Jesus is like a wise person who built his house on a rock. No storm can overthrow that house (Matt. 8:24-27). That is true. A person or society that does not embrace Jesus' ethical foundations experiences cracks and erosion.

For example, consider the call of Jesus to marital fidelity and sexual chastity. Modern sexual permissiveness sows seeds of sorrow and broken homes. And in recent times we have discovered that sexual infidelity is a primary cause for the spread of AIDS.

Another example is Jesus' teachings about avoiding greed and giving generously to the poor. A society or person who lives greedily exploits the poor and creates the social atmosphere where corruption thrives. Such attitudes and practices strangle wholesome business enterprise and development.

Indeed, Sermon-on-the-Mount ethics are a healthy foundation for any society. I was recently a guest in a country where there is about one Christian for every million people.

A local speaker said, "A society that is salted by people who seek to live by the ethical teachings of Jesus is greatly blessed. For example, integrity. In my country there is no assumption that one should practice integrity. The lack of integrity is a debilitating disease in my country."

This does not mean that Christians are the only people who live with integrity. Indeed not! There are Christians who are not honest; not all who claim to believe in Jesus Christ obey his commands. And there are non-Christian people in every society who live righteously and with integrity.

Mahatma Gandhi of India is a noteworthy example. He was a powerful and disturbing mid-twentieth century challenge to the Western church. Gandhi, a Hindu, pled with Western Christians to embrace the teachings of the Sermon on the Mount. He attempted to do so, especially in his nonviolent confrontation with the British enemies of Indian independence.

Ethical "salt" is present whenever people are present in a society who live righteously, whether they are Christians or not.

However, Jesus expects his followers to be "salt" in their society. So does the world. Societies around the world expect people who claim to be Christians to be righteous people; it is a disappointment when they fail to meet such expectations. The late Ayatollah Khomeini, the leader of the Iranian Muslim Revolution, told a church leader who is an acquaintance of mine, "Encourage Christians to obey the teachings of Jesus!"

The ethics of Jesus provide attitudes and conduct that greatly enhance joyful and abundant life. Even though we might believe that, most of us squirm uncomfortably when we hear Jesus exclaim, "Be perfect, therefore, as your heavenly Father is perfect" (Matt. 5:48).

There is a large hospital in Lancaster, Pennsylvania, where my wife Grace helped as a chaplain. The hospital threw a Christmas party. We went. Entertainers provided dinnertime hilarity. Many songs and jokes were about unwholesome attitudes and actions, especially related to sex. There was much laughter, but little or no joy. The hilarity could not overcome the inner sadness and emptiness the vulgarity created.

Nevertheless, multitudes of Christians ignore the Sermon on the Mount, preferring to flow with the joyless norms, attitudes, and vulgarity of their culture and society. In the majority of churches across the United States it is very rare indeed to hear a sermon based on the ethical teachings of Jesus' Sermon on the Mount. Not only the Sermon on the Mount, but all the teachings of Jesus are ignored by many of our acquaintances. What a calamity in an age of moral relativism.

Jesus invites us to an alternative way. He invites us to a good news way of ethical living that is touched with joy.

The Scandal of Forgiveness

Unfortunately, in our sinfulness, we fail. No one has achieved the righteous attitudes and practices Jesus describes, even though we might believe that he is right. For all of us who agree with Jesus that we should be and live the way he taught, the Sermon on the Mount reveals that we need forgiveness. (We also need the empowerment of God to live according to these life enhancing ethical principles. Chapter 10 will explore the power of God that is available for us.)

We observe that Jesus offered the forgiveness people needed. His insistence that he had the authority to forgive sins gave some theologians heartburn.

It is lunacy for me to forgive sins, unless I am forgiving a person for an offense against me. For example, a neighborhood drunk drove into my white birch tree and smashed my good neighbor's car standing in his driveway. I could forgive the drunk driver for breaking my birch tree. Had I then told the drunk that I also forgave him for smashing my neighbor's car, I would have been a candidate for psychiatric care.

"Only God can forgive sins!" theologians fumed. They were right. That was exactly the point Jesus was making; he had the authority to forgive sins.

To forgive and have authority to forgive is costly. Imagine a mother forgiving someone who has tortured and murdered her son. That would be a pain filled commitment. Even God does not short cut the pain, suffering, and tremendous cost that authentic forgiveness requires. Chapter 9 will explore the agony Jesus embraced in his commitment to forgive.

The authority to forgive is costly for any of us who chooses to forgive a person who has sinned against us. The thing that scandalized Israel's theological community was that Jesus exercised that costly authority to forgive sins of anyone who sought forgiveness. The theologians insisted that only God possesses that authority.

I read about a man who demanded sex from a teenage girl. She refused, so he shot and killed her. This happened in the context of battlefield warfare, so he was not prosecuted. Yet his guilt was destroying him.

He sought help from psychiatrists, but none could help him. No psychiatrist can heal that guilt. His friends could not help him, for there is no restitution possible for that crime. Wisely, one of the psychiatrists sent him to a church, for he knew that only God can forgive and heal such guilt. That is the only way.

Students sometimes ask, "But what authority does God have to forgive? Shooting that girl was a crime against her, not against God?" Whoa! Throughout the Bible God makes it clear that all sin and wrong doing is fundamentally sin against God himself. God is the God of righteousness and justice. We are all his beloved children. He is personally affected and wounded by any injustice against anyone of us.

Each person on earth is God's beloved child. Every injustice against one of God's children is an offense against God. God our heavenly Father has ultimate authority to embrace the pain and forgive the wickedness done against any one of his children.

Jesus expressed that authority. He boldly forgave people for the sins they had committed against other people. Not just once. Again and again he forgave people for all their sins, all of them. In his forgiveness, he also commanded, "Go now and leave your life of sin" (John 8:11).

On one occasion friends of a paralytic could not bring their friend close to Jesus because the house was so crowded. So they took away a portion of the roof, and lowered the man with ropes right at Jesus' feet.

Jesus' instant response was, "Son, your sins are forgiven."

When theologians objected, Jesus responded by saying that he would now prove he had authority to forgive sins by healing the man.

"Get up, roll up your mat, and go home!" Jesus commanded.

The paralytic obeyed. He left that house a forgiven man, also cured of his paralysis. The common people were amazed and thankful (Luke 5:17-26).

Who is Jesus?

Only God can forgive sins. Who then is this forgiving Jesus? The alternatives in Jesus' day are the same ones we still face:

1. Jesus is a lunatic.
2. Jesus is a demonized egomaniac.
3. Jesus is God with us, the Son of God.

The only alternative, consistent with the person of Jesus, is that he is indeed the Son of the Living God. The choice is ours, to accept or reject the obvious.

I read *Mere Christianity* by C. S. Lewis in my first year in graduate school, when immersed in the skepticism and unbelief of our culture. I share a statement from Lewis's pen that has remained with me ever since.

> A man who was merely a man and said the sort of things Jesus said would not be a great moral teacher. He would either be a lunatic—on the level with the man who says he is a poached egg—or else he would be the Devil of Hell. You must make your choice. Either this man was, and is, the Son of God; or else a madman or something worse.[5]

Jesus was completely candid about these alternatives. People did deride him for demon possession, which was a catchall term for various forms of lunacy (John 8:48, 52). He faced these charges head on.

"I am not possessed by a demon, but I honor my Father" Jesus countered (John 8:49).

"I and the Father are one!" Jesus insisted (John 10:30). "Anyone who has seen me has seen the Father" (John 14:9).

He declared, If you have any doubts about who I am, just look at my life and ministry and you will see the truth. Accept the witness of the Old Testament Scriptures (John 5:31-47; 8:48-51; 14:11). Despite whatever people might say or think, Jesus declared, "All authority in heaven and on earth has been given to me" (Matt. 28:18).

They crucified Jesus for his outrageous claims. The night of his trial, the core issue of his authority and identity was on everyone's mind. Jesus remained silent as charges were hurled at him. Finally the high priest put it to Jesus bluntly, "Are you the Christ, the Son of the Blessed One?"

Then Jesus spoke.

"I am," said Jesus. "And you will see the Son of man sitting at the right hand of the Mighty One and coming on the clouds of heaven" (Mark 14:61,62).

• • •

Jesus made astounding claims at his trial! "The Son of the Blessed One!" "The Son of man Sitting at the right hand of the Mighty One and coming on the clouds of heaven!" However, these exceedingly amazing claims are consistent with his whole life vocation. These powerful claims by Jesus bring us face to face with the most fundamental question of human existence. Who is God? Who is Jesus?

Students at Lithuania Christian College sometimes say, "We cannot believe in God because we have never seen God. To believe we must see God and know who he is." Jesus is astounding. He claims that when we meet him we have also met God. Can it be true that the God of the whole universe is like Jesus, that Jesus and God are one?

In my prayers, I am honest with God about this. I share with God, "If you are not like Jesus, then I prefer to walk through life without you; I would rather just ignore you.

"However, my Father God, I believe the astonishing good news that Jesus is the fullness of your presence with us. I believe that when I meet Jesus I am also meeting you. I therefore joyfully say yes to you. I am delighted that you are like Jesus!"

I also pray to Jesus, "You are the only figure in history I want to confess as Lord, for in you I have met the only person who has ever loved me totally. I live in daily surprise and wonder, that you, Jesus Christ, are Lord of all! I am delighted!"

8

THE COLT RIDER

Background Scripture: Luke 19:28-48

Jerusalem was in an uproar!

A rabbi from Nazareth was riding a colt into town.

A man riding a young colt into downtown Jerusalem was as routine 2,000 years ago as it is in Old City Jerusalem today. But no one in Jerusalem thought this donkey-riding episode was routine. Some were shouting and singing with joy and others fuming with rage. The city was in tumult. Jesus of Nazareth was riding a colt into Jerusalem!

Why the uproar? A bit of background unlocks the mystery.

At Last: The Son of David!

It was a thousand years before this colt-riding event that the Prophet Nathan had given King David the message from God saying, "Your house and your kingdom will endure forever before me; your throne will be established forever" (2 Sam. 7:16). (See Chapter 6.) However, tragically for nearly 600 years, no king had sat on David's throne, for Israel had no king.

The Babylonians had crushed Jerusalem in 586 B.C. King Zedekiah was reigning; he was the culmination of twenty-one generations of kings descended from King David. Zedekiah was arrested. King Nebuchadnezzar of Babylon pronounced judgment. Zedekiah's sons were killed in his presence, then his eyes were plucked. The last thing he saw was the death of his sons.

This was a personal calamity. It was also a national catastrophe. King Zedekiah and Israel had hoped that one of his sons would continue David's kingly line. They anticipated that sometime a descendant of David would fulfill God's promise to King David by reigning forever and establishing an eternal kingdom.

For the next six centuries Israel hoped that God would even yet fulfill his promise to David. There were a number of families in Israel who in their various family trees traced their genealogy to King David. That hope of a king from David's line establishing an eternal kingdom persisted against all odds. The last of the Old Testament biblical prophets, Malachi, wrote about that hope; so did visionaries such as the Essenes, who practiced religious piety in the nearby deserts. Malachi (c.433 B.C.) proclaimed this hope in winsome metaphor, saying that "the sun of righteousness will rise with healing in its wings. And you will go out and leap like calves released from the stall" (Mal. 4:2).

Communities such as the Essenes also nurtured the hope, as revealed in the Dead Sea Scrolls. A young Arab shepherd discovered these scrolls in 1947 in desert caves in Palestine near the Dead Sea. These parchments reveal that, even after Malachi, the hope persisted that God would fulfill his promise to David. They wrote in expectation about the rule of the King of Righteousness. Their writings anticipated the Messiah who would be called the Son of the Most High. He would establish peace. What a strange and impossible hope it all seemed to be.[1]

There were some heroic efforts from time to time to reestablish Jewish rule in Jerusalem and the surrounding region. Most noteworthy was nearly 130 years of Maccabee rule (166-37 B.C.). However, the Maccabees were priests; they were not kings from David's line. They did not rule forever, nor were they celebrated for their righteousness. They could not be the fulfillment of God's promise to King David; neither were the scheming violent Herods who subsequently ruled Israel as puppets of the Roman Empire.

Why Ride a Colt?

However, when Jesus, the rabbi from Nazareth, rode into the city on a colt, the foundations of Jerusalem society quaked. He was proclaiming that he was the King from David's line! Probably every Sabbath school child in Jerusalem had memorized a little Scripture verse tucked in among the writings of the prophets. This was what the Prophet Zechariah had written five hundred years earlier.

> Rejoice greatly, O Daughter of Zion!
>> Shout, daughter of Jerusalem!
> See, your king comes to you,
>> righteous and having salvation,
> gentle and riding on a donkey
>> on a colt, the foal of a donkey. . . . (Zech. 9:9)

By riding that colt, Jesus was announcing that he was the fulfillment of Zechariah's prophecy. He was proclaiming that he was inaugurating the promise of God to King David. Jesus was revealing that the kingdom he was establishing would be different from all others. Other kings rode on horses or in chariots, signs of power. Jesus rode a colt, a poor man's transport. The gentleness and persistence of the colt was a sign of this king's gentle authority.

The children of Jerusalem were especially exhilarated that day. They loved Jesus. Stories of his enjoyment of children and his blessing the children had likely circulated throughout the land. We imagine the oral grapevine taking the news from Dan in the north to Beersheba in the south, as people told of Jesus calling the children to come to him and saying,

> Let the little children come to me, and do not hinder them, for the kingdom of God belongs to such as these. I tell you the truth, anyone who will not receive the kingdom of God like a little child will never enter it. (Mark 10:14-15)

So with great joy the children sang as they danced along with Jesus on the colt,

> Hosanna to the son of David!
> Blessed is he who comes in the name
>   of the Lord!
> Hosanna in the highest! (Matt. 21:9)

The throngs had no red carpet to place on the pavement to honor the King riding that colt. So they put their garments on the pavement, and waved palm leaves as they sang.

The religious authorities were furious. They demanded that Jesus order the children to be silent. They were outraged at the presumption of Jesus to ride that colt into Jerusalem.

They muttered in rage: Jesus is only a deluded teacher, not a king. The promised king will be of David's royal line, born in Bethlehem, the same city from which David came. This Jesus, the carpenter from Nazareth, cannot be the promised King.

But Jesus would not silence the jubilation. He astounded the authorities by exclaiming, "If they keep quiet, the stones will cry out!"

Probably unknown to the authorities, Jesus of Nazareth had been born in Bethlehem, just as Micah (5:2) had promised and as everyone who has heard the account of Jesus' birth knows (Luke 2:1-7). At his birth, this king's bed was a manger for cattle. Angels announced his birth to shepherds; a star announced his birth to wise men from nations far to the east. His mother, the virgin Mary, and Joseph who later married Mary, traced their lineage to King David. (Matt.1:1-17 and Luke 3:23-38 each in their varying ways trace the lineage.)

Nevertheless, these "facts" and "events" were unnoticed and irrelevant, as far as the authorities were concerned. They were appalled that Jesus was declaring that he was the King. He was most definitely not the kind of king they wanted.

The children dancing and singing "Hosanna" in the streets of Jerusalem probably did not know the significance of the verse that follows the prophet Zechariah's announcement that the King would ride a colt. But the leaders of the religious community well knew the next sentence. So did Jesus. Those verses are an astonishing proclamation.

Zechariah wrote,

> He will proclaim peace to the nations.
> His rule will extend from sea to sea
> and from the River to the ends of the earth.
> (Zech. 9:10)

By riding that colt, Jesus proclaimed that he would establish a kingdom extending throughout the earth. Earlier that day, when Jesus had asked two of his assistants to find a colt, and bring it to him for a ride into Jerusalem, he well knew what he was doing. Jesus intended to reveal in this gentle and quite ordinary act that he was inaugurating God's universal kingdom that will extend from nation to nation all around the world.

Many people assume that Jesus never intended to establish a universal church or kingdom. They believe that the church has vastly overstated Jesus' intentions. That is what all of my Muslim friends say. So do many others with whom I converse, including some biblical scholars.

Such notions try to place Jesus into a box that limits his authority. However, by riding that colt, Jesus was intentionally and boldly proclaiming that he was indeed the promised king, who would extend his rule, not only in Israel, but to all nations. His kingdom would be eternal and universal.

Peace Is a Gift Offered

Jesus approached Jerusalem that day from the Mount of Olives lying to the east of the city. He paused on his colt on that Mount overlooking Jerusalem, and began weeping. What a contrast! Jubilant hosannas. Angry authorities. A weeping Jesus. Then, just before Jesus began the descent into the city, he told those around him the reason for his tears.

Jesus said, as he gazed at the city below him,

If you, even you, had only known on this day what would bring you peace—but now it is hidden from your eyes. The days will come upon you when your enemies will build an embankment against you and encircle you and hem you in on every side. They will dash you to the ground, you and the children within your walls. They will not leave one stone on another, because you did not recognize the time of God's coming to you. (Luke 19:41-44)

What a paradox. On the very day Jesus reveals he is the King who will extend his rule of peace to the nations, he weeps because Jerusalem will not receive his peace. The peace Jesus offers is a gift to be received or rejected. Jesus proclaims peace but never forces the peace. He proclaims peace to the nations; he does not force peace on either Jerusalem or the nations.

Herein is one of the great differences between the kingdom Jesus establishes and other kingdoms. The kingdom Jesus invites us into is voluntary. There is no compulsion. There are no inducements or enticements. The gift of peace is offered; the invitation is extended; we then decide.

Jesus entered Jerusalem that day with no symbols of earthly power. He did not even ride a donkey; he chose a colt, the foal of a donkey, the most fragile animal able to carry him. He rode gently. The peace he offered Jerusalem that day was an invitation given with tears, just that.

Other Kinds of Peace

Islam also offers a kingdom of peace. Six centuries after Jesus rode the colt into Jerusalem, Mohammed entered Mecca, which is the Jerusalem of the Muslim people. Before entering Mecca, Mohammed had defeated the Meccan armies in battles. He entered Mecca as a victorious general to extend the peace of Islam throughout that city.

In four centuries after Christ, the Christian church also sought to establish and sometimes extend God's kingdom through political and military means. This was especially true in Europe. The difficulty arose when the Roman Emperor, Constantine, began to bring the church and empire into a very intimate relationship. Historians refer to this process as the "Constantinization" of the church. At times he used the military to support the goals of the church.

During the next several centuries a process began so that eventually the political authorities throughout Europe determined that all their citizens should be Christians. Membership in the church and citizenship were identical. The practice of baptizing all babies as Christians helped to establish that reality. There was no choice, for everyone in a Christian state was baptized as a Christian. People who did not submit to the authority of the church were often persecuted or even killed. Violent extension or protection of the church continued in various ways for many centuries.

For example, in 1099 Christian armies from western Europe invaded Jerusalem. They fought and defeated the Muslims and established a so-called Christian kingdom.

Both Islam and the Constantinian church used similar means to extend their different visions of the kingdom of God. Not only did Muslims and Christians fight one another, but Muslims sometimes fought Muslims, and Christians likewise fought against each other. They fought to defend their different understandings of God's kingdom and his peace.

Only for Volunteers!

Not so Jesus. Jesus proclaimed God's peace peacefully. He entered Jerusalem riding a colt. Those who enter the kingdom he leads are all volunteers; no one is present because she has been forced to enter the kingdom.

That was the commitment of the first Christians and the early church. They believed that God's kingdom is the peaceable kingdom. In later centuries in Europe, back to the Bible re-newal movements such as the Waldenses (twelfth century) called on the western church to turn away from embracing world-like power and walk in the way of Jesus Christ. Likewise the Anabaptists of the sixteenth century sought to commit themselves to the kingdom of this colt-riding King Jesus.

The Waldenses and Anabaptists believed that followers of Jesus should be peacemaking volunteers. Neither the church nor the state had the authority to require faith or participation in the kingdom of God. For this reason they called for baptism of adults who had voluntarily chosen to say yes to Jesus Christ.

The church state authorities were terrified. They knew that baptizing adults rather than children would shatter the whole church state system in sixteenth century Europe. Adult baptism was a revolutionary statement for freedom of conscience. It laid the foundation for the free church movement in Europe.

Groups such as the Waldenses, or Anabaptists were the pio-neers of the free church movement in Europe. Free churches function independently of the state church system. The free churches include denominations such as the Methodists, Bap-tists, Moravians, Quakers, Pentecostals, Mennonites, the Breth-ren, and a variety of new denominations that have emerged in recent years.

The commitment to adult rather than infant baptism chal-lenged and helped to fragment the foundations of sixteenth century European political and religious life, thereby providing room for personal freedom of conscience and the emergence of free churches. This freedom also meant that the person is free to reject faith and the church.

Churches throughout the world today largely agree that the choice to follow Jesus should be a voluntary choice. Even churches that baptize babies have a confirmation later when the young person declares his faith commitment. The church is a community of volunteers. However, these volunteers need to resist being proud of their decision to be a Christian. The New

Testament reveals that it is God who invites us to say yes to Jesus. He calls, through his Holy Spirit, working through the Scriptures, the church, our circumstances, or in other ways.

God respects our freedom to choose; he does not force us to believe. Although the choice to believe or not to believe is our responsibility, it is God who plants in the soul of a person the conviction and the desire to say yes to Jesus Christ.

An Amazing Kind of King

Amid all the tumult in Jerusalem when Jesus rode the colt into town, Christians believe God was at work encouraging people to believe in Jesus and receive the peace that he offers. Nevertheless, the city was profoundly divided about Jesus, just as it is true today in every community where Jesus is known. Some choose to believe in Jesus, and others reject him.

Jesus could have ridden into Jerusalem on a gallant stallion at the head of an army, like victorious generals do, or like the Christian crusaders did who invaded Jerusalem in the eleventh century. Most people would have understood and most likely followed that kind of king.

In fact, on one occasion fans of Jesus tried to make him become their king. Throngs of people had surrounded Jesus in Galilee in the northern hills wanting to force him to become their king (John 6:15). This is the region where Zealot freedom fighters were waging hit-and-run-battles against the Roman occupation.

Just before this incident, Jesus had just fed 5,000 men, plus women and children, through the miraculous multiplication of five loaves of bread and two fishes. Everyone was impressed! People recognized that with Jesus as their king, the logistical difficulties of providing food for the freedom fighters would be resolved immediately. Jesus could feed all the soldiers miraculously.

It is likely that all of the freedom fighters would have joined Jesus if he had accepted the demand to become king. With Jesus as their commander, they could take Jerusalem and throw out the hated Roman rulers.

Even much more impressive than leading a human army into Jerusalem, Jesus could have marshaled an army of angels. He told his disciples that if he asked God for the help of angels, God would instantly send him an army of 12 legions (Matt. 26:53). That would be a force of up to 72,000 angels.

Jesus never asked God to send a battalion of angels as he entered Jerusalem. Neither did he accept the invitation, some months earlier, to become the king of the Galilean throngs leading their military units. Instead, he slipped away from the Galileans, and went into the mountains to pray alone (John 6:15, Matthew 14:23). When he rejoined his followers, he told them that the time was coming soon when he will be crucified (Luke 9:22). Thereafter, he began the deliberate journey from Galilee to Jerusalem, where he told his followers that his crucifixion would take place (Luke 9:51; 18:31-33).

Jesus' followers were utterly perplexed. Why would the one who they were sure was the promised King, refuse the offer to become king? Why was he setting his face to go to Jerusalem where he would be crucified?

The disciples of Jesus did not understand. Sometimes they listened to Jesus in painful or perplexed silence. Sometimes they openly confronted Jesus. A crucified king was just wrong, if not totally crazy. A crucified Jesus would be a powerless king. No peace could come from such a king!

Nevertheless, Jesus proclaims peace. He does not force anyone to accept the peace he offers. He does not extend the peace through military or even angelic force. His peace is a gift offered, never a peace coerced. His is a costly peace, a peace revealed and established in his crucifixion.

The next chapter will explore the relationship of the crucifixion to the peace Jesus offers. For the present we note just this: the choice is ours. Jesus wept that day as he looked over Jerusalem. He wept because he knew that the choices of that city in the days ahead would turn Jerusalem away from King Jesus and true peace.

A Costly Confrontation

Jesus rode that colt right up to the temple. The children followed him into the temple court still singing, "Hosanna to the Son of David!" The temple rulers were beside themselves with dismay. However, rather than quiet the children as they entered the house of God, Jesus encouraged their singing by exclaiming with appreciation, "From the lips of children and infants you have ordained praise" (Matt. 21:16).

The events of that tumultuous day in Jerusalem were not yet over. Jesus strode into the temple courts where merchants operated a market for those who came to the temple for worship. That market was a symptom of a religious system that exploited the poor.

These merchants were occupying the temple area that was especially reserved for visitors from other nations, the Gentiles. However, the merchants had occupied the visitors section, creating a market place atmosphere in the area that was intended for prayer and the teaching of God's Word to those who came from distant lands.

It is not surprising that Jesus was angry. He exclaimed, quoting from the Scriptures,

> Is it not written:
> "My house will be called
>   a house of prayer for all nations?"
> But you have made it
>   "a den of robbers." (Mark 11:17)

At this time 18,000 people were employed by the temple system; most rotated into Jerusalem and then back to the countryside in regular work details. There were at least two dozen Jewish taxes imposed to keep the temple and religious systems functioning. The taxes to support the system were heavy; between Roman and Jewish taxes, the people paid between forty percent and seventy percent in taxes annually. The temple market overcharged the worshipers who might need a dove or a lamb for sacrifice. The people in the system benefited, but for many the costly temple was a burden.[2]

Jesus walked into the market, and with a whip chased the cattle and sheep from the area. He overturned the money tables with coins scattering everywhere. He chased all the merchants out into the streets. The temple authorities were furious.

The Wrong Kind of People

The uproar Jesus created in Jerusalem was not the first time that he had astonished everyone and appalled many. In fact, only a day or two before his colt ride into Jerusalem, Jesus had also left Jericho in uproar. Jericho was a city in the Jordan Valley that Jesus walked through on his journey to Jerusalem. Jesus entered the city acclaimed as a real hero; he left the city denounced as a traitor.

This is what happened.

On the eastern outskirts of Jericho, a blind beggar, Bartimaeus, raised his voice above the throngs walking with Jesus. He shouted boldly, "Jesus, Son of David, have mercy on me" (Luke 18:35-43).

The crowds tried to silence Bartimaeus, but he just shouted more obnoxiously. Jesus heard him, called for him, and healed him of his blindness. The crowds were electrified with delight and praised God. By the time Jesus got into the center of the town, the surprising good news about Bartimaeus had spread everywhere, and throngs crowded the roadway to see Jesus.

Then Jesus met Zacchaeus (Luke 19:1-10). Kenneth Bailey, who has lived in the Middle East for many years, interprets what happened from the perspective of the natives of Jericho.[3]

Zacchaeus was a traitor to the people of Jericho. He collected taxes for the hated Roman occupation. He over-taxed. The Romans required a set annual tax from Zacchaeus. Anything he could collect above the Roman requirements, Zacchaeus pocketed. Zacchaeus squeezed unfair taxes from the community. He became wealthy at their expense. He was involved in legalized robbery. As far as the locals were concerned, Zacchaeus was a traitor and a robber.

The one rule a person such as Zacchaeus had to live by was this; avoid crowds. In a crowd, an anonymous person could stealthily slip a dagger or knife from its sheath and quite silently plunge it into the abdomen of the hated traitor. No one would know who did it. Or a crowd might simply go berserk at the sight of the traitor and lynch him. Avoid crowds. Zacchaeus knew that rule well.

Nevertheless, Zacchaeus wanted to see Jesus. He was an officer, employed by the Roman government. Although short of stature, he could demand the right to walk through the crowd and stand in front of everyone, and see Jesus from the front row. That was expected of officials. But that approach would not be wise, for crowds were dangerous.

Zacchaeus developed another strategy. He slipped unnoticed to the western edge of the city, away from the clamor in the city-center. He climbed a tree, a most undignified thing for a Roman officer to do. But he felt safe and well hidden among the leaves; no one had seen him.

Or so he thought. Perhaps some children spied him climbing their favorite tree. In any event, the word swept that crowd; Zacchaeus was in the tree at the end of town. Like dogs after a raccoon, a large crowd ran and gathered around that tree. The mob was delighted. At last Zacchaeus was treed. They would get him, now. Mob justice would make it impossible for the Roman authorities in town to arrest anyone. All would participate in the lynching.

Jesus saw what was happening ahead along the roadside on the western edge of town. When he got to the tree, he pushed through the hate-crazed crowd. Then Jesus called, "Zacchaeus, come down immediately. I must stay at your house today."

In that invitation, Jesus saved Zacchaeus' life. Zacchaeus was overjoyed. The crowds were appalled. All the people muttered against Jesus in dismay and disgust.

The change in mood was utterly dramatic. When Jesus healed blind Bartimaeus on the eastern edge of town, the throngs were overjoyed giving thanks to God. However, on the western side, "all the people" were muttering against Jesus who had befriended the traitor, Zacchaeus. Who is this unpredictable "Son of David"? He just did not fit their expectations.

At that dinner Zacchaeus stood up and said, "Look, Lord! Here and now I give half of my possessions to the poor, and if I have cheated anybody out of anything, I will pay back four times the amount."

Jesus responded, "Today salvation has come to this house, because this man, too, is a son of Abraham. For the Son of man came to seek and to save what was lost" (Luke 19:8-10).

The Wrong Kind of King

By the time Jesus had walked the 20 miles from Jericho up to Jerusalem, the Jewish authorities had surely heard of the unthinkable impropriety of Jesus requesting hospitality in the home of a traitor like Zachaeus. The king they were looking for would condemn such traitors, not eat with them.

Jesus was not the kind of king the authorities in Jerusalem wanted. His presumptions, confrontations, and friendships were upsetting their whole world. Jesus was dangerous.

It was not only the authorities who determined that Jesus must die. One of his own disciples, Judas Iscariot, came to the same conclusion. Early on in his ministry, Jesus had appointed twelve men to be his companions or disciples. Judas Iscariot was probably the only one of these disciples from Judea, the area surrounding Jerusalem; the others came from Galilee in the northern part of the country.

By the time Jesus had arrived in Jerusalem, Judas had determined that Jesus was not his kind of king. Judas went to the authorities, and made a deal; they gave him about $20. Judas promised to lead their soldiers to an easy late night arrest of Jesus when Jerusalem was asleep.

The evening of the planned arrest, Jesus and his disciples were in an upper room eating the Jewish Passover meal together. It was a sad meal. The disciples were arguing about who was the greatest among them. Jesus had discerned that Judas was planning to betray him. Jesus was always straightforward, and announced that a betrayal was at hand, and made it quite clear indeed who was involved.

Then in an act of astonishing servant love, Jesus left his place at the dinner table, got a basin with water and a towel, and began washing the feet of each disciple (John 13:1-17). The seating arrangement that night indicates that he began to wash the feet of Judas Iscariot first.

Imagine that!

The colt riding king washed the feet of each disciple; that was the work of a slave or servant, not a king. Jesus washed the feet of Judas Iscariot that sad night. I suppose Jesus might have shed tears of compassion for Judas; I imagine his salty tears mingling with water in that basin. However, Judas would not be swayed from his intentions. Judas would not accept Jesus as king. He slipped away from the Passover meal to arrange for the arrest.

Late that evening Judas led the soldiers to where Jesus was praying with a few disciples nearby, in the Garden of Gethsemane just east of Jerusalem. Terrified, one of his disciples wielded a sword in an attempt to protect Jesus from the arresting officers.

Jesus rebuked the disciple.

At his late night trial Jesus said to Pilate, the Roman governor, "My kingdom is not of this world. If it were, my servants would fight to prevent my arrest by the Jews. But now my kingdom is from another place."

"You are a king, then!" said Pilate.

Jesus answered, "You are right in saying I am a king. In fact, for this reason I was born, and for this I came into the world, to testify to the truth. Everyone on the side of truth listens to me" (John 18:36-37).

The arresting authorities derided Jesus for claiming to be king. Soldiers placed a crown of thorns on his head. They put a kingly robe on him. They spat in his face and whipped and slapped him.

In derision, the Roman authorities wrote an inscription on the cross above his head. "The King of the Jews," the sign announced in Latin, Greek, and Aramaic (John 19:19).

• • •

A king riding a colt! What a delightful surprise, and the children just loved it all.

Even in these modern times, once a year in churches around the world, congregations celebrate the surprise and joy of that day when Jesus rode into Jerusalem on a colt. This festive event is called Palm Sunday, the week before Easter, when the church celebrates the resurrection of Christ. Children wave palms and sing Hosannas to King Jesus.

What a surprise. Jesus is a radically different king than all others. His army of occupation as he entered Jerusalem was singing, joyful, dancing children. This King astonished his disciples by washing their feet, a job that only a servant would do. He even washed the feet of the man who betrayed him. This king was crucified on a cross on the outskirts of Jerusalem, and those who directed the crucifixion put a sign over his head: The King of the Jews.

We are astounded. Can this crucified Jesus really be King? Yet today we observe that the kingdom of peace this King proclaimed extends throughout the world. Though of course it is often shadowed by worldly evil, it is present in every nation. His kingdom possesses no army or systems to enforce its power. It is a movement of volunteers who gather in regular worship remembering that Jesus, their King, was crucified, and that they are called to suffer and love as he did. remembering that Jesus, their King, was crucified, and that they are called to suffer and love as he did.

A cross is present in most churches, a reminder that Jesus was crucified. The next chapter will explore the meaning of the crucifixion of Jesus in God's plan to establish David's kingdom forever.

9

THE LAMB
AND THE SCROLL

Background Scripture: Revelation 5
John wept and wept!
He cried because no one was worthy to take the scroll.
Then to his astonishment, a Lamb took the scroll.
(A scroll is a long narrow sheet of parchment containing writing. A scroll can be rolled together tightly.)
John's sorrow was transformed into joy when he saw the Lamb taking the scroll. What a strange and surprising vision. What can it mean?
This vision of the Lamb with the scroll is described in Revelation 5. The language is metaphorical. These word pictures open our understanding to the meaning of history and the nature of power.
Revelation is the last book of the Bible. It is different than most of the Bible because it is a vision, somewhat like a dream. Most of the Bible is quite different than Revelation, for it is rooted in historical events and the writings of prophets who interpret and proclaim the meaning of God's acts in history. However, Revelation is a vision, and what we read here is like a painting that communicates many surprises.
John, who wrote Revelation, was an exile on the rocky, barren island of Patmos. This small island is about fifty miles off the

southwest coast of modern Turkey. It was there on Patmos that John saw a vision of God on his throne. God had a scroll in his hand, written on both sides and sealed with seven seals.

This scroll is a metaphor of our human situation. Our story is inscribed in that scroll. Our sinfulness is also hidden in that scroll. The scroll is sealed so that what is inside will remain a secret. The only one worthy to open that scroll is the one able to redeem us from our sinfulness, the one who can deal with all the secrets locked inside that scroll, the one who can give meaning to life.

The Search Goes Everywhere

John observed that a search began to find the one who was worthy to take the scroll of our history into his authority. They searched in heaven, on Earth, and under the earth. They found no one, however, who was worthy to take the scroll.

That search for someone worthy to take the scroll continues today. There are many who volunteer to take the scroll—people or authorities who want to direct and control our lives. These authorities announce that they can rescue us from sinfulness and evil.

Many religions seek to claim the scroll. That has been the mission of militant Islam as it seeks to impose Islamic rule on societies wherever possible. In the United States, some Christian organizations have aligned with either a conservative or a liberal political agenda to save America. Bosnian Christians have tried to force their version of Christian hegemony on Bosnia and the Muslims. In India the Bharatiya Janata Party (BJP) has sought to make India into a Hindu state. These are examples of religious authorities who seek to control human history and destiny. However, the consequence of such efforts by the religions to control human destiny is tragic.

Ideologies and political systems also lay claim to the destiny of humanity. The twentieth century has experienced colossal conflicts as ideologies have tried to seize the scroll of human history and destiny. That has been the Marxist agenda throughout much of the twentieth century. Likewise Hitler's Nazi Germany claimed the right of the Aryan race to rule all other races. The "self-evident" truth of American democracy has nurtured the conviction that America has a "manifest destiny" to spread its ideals around the world. Such ideologies have plunged the world into the most horrible wars in human history.

As the search continued, John wept, because no one was worthy to take control of human destiny. Around the world today there is, likewise, a touch of deep grief everywhere as we discern that no one is worthy to take the scroll, for no one is capable of redeeming us from our sinfulness and death.

The Awesome Surprise

Then came the wonderful surprise.

An elder said to John, "Stop weeping! Look! Someone has been found worthy to take the scroll!"

"Who is worthy?" John wondered.

"He's the Lion of Judah, the Root of David!" the elder exclaimed.

These are names for the Messiah, who is Jesus. The previous chapter explored ministries of Jesus as the promised King from David's line; he is the Root of David. David was from the clan of Judah in the nation of Israel. Jesus, from the clan of Judah, is like a lion, capable, strong, and victorious. Through the use of these names the messenger was informing John that Jesus was the only one worthy and capable to take the scroll.

However, as John peered into heaven, he did not see a king or a lion, although all those descriptions are true of Jesus. The picture of Jesus he saw was "a Lamb, looking as if it had been slain, standing in the center of the throne" (Rev. 5:6).

The Lamb took the scroll!

A New Song

Joy cascaded through heaven and earth as the Lamb took the scroll. The choirs of heaven sang a new song.

> You are worthy to take the scroll
> > and to open its seals,
> because you were slain,
> > and with your blood
> you purchased men for God
> > from every tribe and language and
> > people and nation.
> You have made them to be a kingdom
> > and priests to serve our God
> and they will reign on the earth. (Rev. 5:9-10)
> Then over a billion angels joined in the choir singing,
> Worthy is the Lamb, who was slain
> > to receive power and wealth and
> wisdom and strength
> > and honor and glory and praise! (Rev. 5:12)

Then every creature in heaven and earth sang with overflowing joy. That must have included crickets, crocodiles, giraffes, whales, storks, and all other creatures. All were delighted that the Lamb had the scroll, and they sang,

> To him who sits on the throne and
> > to the lamb
> be praise and honor and glory and power,
> > forever and ever! (Rev. 5:13)

The Lamb

The Lamb is Jesus. Why is Jesus called the Lamb? Why is he worthy to take the scroll of history in his hands?

At the very beginning of Jesus' public ministry, he went to his friend and relative, John the Baptist. (He is not the same John who saw the vision on Patmos.) At that time, John was preaching along the Jordan River, inviting people to repent and prepare for the coming of the Savior. Jesus went to John for baptism.

As John saw Jesus approaching, he called out, "Look, the Lamb of God who takes away the sin of the world! . . . I testify that this is the Son of God" (John 1:29,34). Why did John link the name, Lamb of God, with the name, Son of God, at the time of Jesus' baptism? The answer to that question helps to unlock the mystery of Jesus' astonishing authority to forgive sins that we encountered in the previous chapter.

We will explore two dimensions of the mystery of Jesus as Lamb of God and Son of God: forgiveness and reconciliation.

Forgiveness

The jury and judge determined that justice requires death for Timothy McVeigh, who was convicted of the 1995 bombing of the federal building in Oklahoma City that killed 168 people. Yet Bud Welch, who lost his daughter in that bombing, reminded us that Jesus said that if a man hits you on one cheek, turn the other. Welch asked that McVeigh not die; he wanted time to forgive McVeigh and time to pray for his redemption.

McVeigh showed no remorse at the trial. Could the court or the judge forgive him? Could the judge suspend the sentence, commute the death penalty, and free McVeigh from prison? Any judge who would take such actions would face impeachment. Neither society nor the legal system could permit McVeigh to escape the penalty for his actions.

Courts function on the premise of justice. A person must pay a penalty for his crime; forgiveness is difficult to fathom. How can a court forgive a crime against another person, especially if restitution is impossible?

Religions likewise struggle with these issues of justice and forgiveness. In a Buddhist sangha in Washington, D.C., a ninety-some-year-old monk became agitated when we asked him, "How can a person find forgiveness for sin?"

"Forgiveness!" he exclaimed. "That is an impossibility. Each person must bear the consequence of his own actions. Notions of forgiveness destroy the moral foundations of society."

Classical Hinduism says the same thing. Your deeds determine your karma. Your karma determines your destiny, like a tennis racket hitting a ball. There can be no forgiveness, only a tallying, as it were, of your good and bad deeds.

I frequently visit mosques. Most often I see a person here and there facing Mecca and going through the prayer *rakas* alone. (A *raka* is the prayer cycle involving standing and kneeling while reciting Arabic prayers.) Whenever I ask, why the extra prayers, the answer is always the same.

"There is a balance scales for each of us. On one side is the good we do. On the other the wrong we commit. Ritual prayers add weight to the good side of the scales. These persons have sinned and they hope God will notice their extra prayers and forgive their sins."

"When have they said enough prayers?" I often ask.

My Muslim friends reply, "We do not know."

Our Muslim friends are right. How many ritual prayers does it take to counterbalance adultery, theft, or deceit? The requirements of justice and the need for forgiveness collide. We all know that is true. That is why classical Hinduism declares boldly that forgiveness is impossible; it is a violation of the fundamental laws of the universe. Forgiveness cannot short circuit justice. The law of justice must be fulfilled. Our courts are based on that conviction.

In my studies of world religions, I am impressed how universal that conviction is; forgiveness cannot circumvent justice. I believe that conviction is stamped in the human soul because we are created in God's image, the God who longs to establish justice throughout the earth. Religious philosophers in systems like orthodox Buddhism or Vedanta Hinduism have despaired of finding any way to reconcile justice and forgiveness. They, therefore, insist that forgiveness is impossible.

However, in the crucified Jesus, justice is fulfilled. He has taken our place. In Jesus Christ, God, the Judge of the universe has entered the court room and taken our place. Scriptures exclaim, "All this is from God, who reconciled us to himself through Christ. . . . God was reconciling the world to himself in Christ, not counting men's sins against them" (2 Cor. 5:18, 19).

Imagine the judge in Timothy Mcveigh's trial announcing that justice required the death penalty for McVeigh. Imagine him rising from his judge's bench and walking over to McVeigh, placing his hand on his shoulder, and saying, "I love you, Timothy. I will take your place. You are free." Imagine that innocent judge facing death by hanging on a tree (the way murders were executed in the American Midwest at one time), while McVeigh walked free.

Take note. McVeigh would have to accept the judge's offer to be free. And the firm expectation of the judge would have to be that McVeigh will leave his life of violence and invest the rest of his days in serving his fellow humans, not destroying them.

This imaginary discourse helps us understand what God has done for us in Jesus Christ. God has given Christ the authority to be our Judge (Matt. 26:31-46). Jesus, our Judge, has entered the courtroom of your life, of my life, and has taken our place. Whatever our sins might be, he has taken our place. The soldiers nailed Jesus Christ to a cross and he died a criminal's death. In his crucifixion, Jesus Christ has taken our place. We are free.

However, we need to receive that gift; otherwise the gift of forgiveness will pass us by. Christ offers the costly gift of forgiveness; we need to receive that gift with thankfulness and repent of our sinful ways. If we are indifferent to Christ's gift of forgiveness or reject that gift, then the gift will not be ours.

In the previous chapter we discovered that the people were amazed that Jesus forgave sins. However, forgiveness is costly. One cannot wave a divine scepter, as it were, and declare people forgiven. God, who is the author of justice, will not abrogate justice to forgive us.

However, Jesus, who is the sinless Son of God, became sin for us (2 Cor. 5:21). That fact gives him authority to forgive sins. He took on himself the death that is the consequence of our sinfulness (1 Pet. 2:24). He died a criminal's death, crucified on a cross, between thieves. No matter what our crime and sin, Jesus Christ has taken our place (1 Pet. 3:18). It is on that basis that he offers forgiveness (Matt. 26:27, 28).

Who needs forgiveness?

McVeigh committed a heinous crime; he needs forgiveness. No one denies that. However, most of us do not have that kind of blood on our hands. In fact, we might feel no need for forgiveness for anything. That was how my friend Mohammed felt. Some years ago, he asked to have a Bible study with me. One evening he said, "It seems that Jesus forgives sinners. Is that true?"

"Yes," I replied. "Isn't that a special surprise?"

"But I am a very good person. I am not a sinner. So I do not need Jesus," he exclaimed.

That was Mohammed's last evening in the Bible study.

Our sense of a need for forgiveness depends on where we put the moral goalposts in our lives. For example, Timothy McVeigh seemed to feel that the Oklahoma City bombing was justified as retaliation against the U.S. government for restricting the freedom of people. It appears that Slobodan Milosevic in his capacity as President of Yugoslavia could not understand why the World Court in the Hague indicted him at the height of the 1999 Kosovo War for war crimes. After all, he was fighting to protect the ethnic purity of Serbs. These might seem extreme examples of moral confusion.

Each of us is inclined to set our moral goalposts at the place in our lives where there will be no challenge to our personal moral commitments. Nevertheless, the biblical Scriptures and Jesus confront us with an alternative: let God set the standards. And God's righteous standards are very good. They also reveal that without exception each of us are sinners in need of God's grace and forgiveness. In the Sermon on the Mount Jesus not only addresses what we do, but he also confronts our inner attitudes like a critical attitude, a greedy spirit, resentment, or pride.

A surprising characteristic of all who walk in Christ's Way is this: they know they are sinners. They rejoice in being forgiven.

Here is an interesting, albeit profound, experiment. Confront a person who has erred with this statement, "You have done wrong." Those who do not know the forgiveness of Christ will most likely surprise you by responding, "I am not a bad person. Others have done worse things than that."

A person who has embraced Christ's forgiveness, will likely surprise you by saying, "That is true. In fact, I have done worse things than that."

Forgiveness frees us from defensiveness and hypocrisy. Forgiven people know "if we claim to be without sin, we deceive ourselves and the truth is not in us. If we confess our sins, he is faithful and just and will forgive us our sins and purify us from all unrighteousness" (1 John 1:8,9).

Forgiveness requires sacrifice

However, the cost of forgiveness is enormous. In the quest for forgiveness, traditional religions universally have offered animals or even humans in sacrifice.

Recall that when Israel was freed from slavery in Egypt, each household sacrificed a lamb and sprinkled the blood above and on the sides of their doors. When the angel of death slew the first born throughout Egypt, those households with the blood of the sacrificed lamb were safe. Animal sacrifices for protection and forgiveness are a widespread practice in the Old Testament and traditional religions everywhere. (We will explore the role of sacrifice more under the theme of reconciliation.)

What is the meaning of this universal phenomenon of animal sacrifices? The biblical New Testament Scriptures proclaim with confidence that Jesus is the sacrifice for our sins. All the animals ever sacrificed in the quest for forgiveness are signs pointing to the one who is the sinless one, the Lamb of God, who has taken our place (Heb. 10:1,10).

Menno Simons, whose name is identified with the Christian Mennonite denomination, wrote,

> The righteous died for the unrighteous, when we were yet sinners and enemies. . . . The innocent One bore the burden of the . . . world . . . for the guilt of all. . . . The Scriptures speak of but one means against my sin, namely of the pure and red blood of my Lord Jesus Christ.

Several years ago my wife and I worshiped with a congregation of recent believers who had become part of a new church planting in Alpha, New Jersey. Church planter Henry Swartley led us in communion (the Eucharist or Lord's supper). We sat in small circles sharing the bread and cup of wine in intimate clusters. The bread and wine are symbols of the body and blood of Jesus offered on the cross as the sacrifice for our sins.

As we shared the cup in my circle, a young woman sat weeping softly. I heard her repeating over and over in a quiet whisper, "Thank you Jesus for dying for my sins. Thank you that I am forgiven. Thank you. Thank you."

All around the world in every society and culture, wherever people repent and receive the costly forgiveness Jesus offers, they are forgiven. They know the joy of forgiveness.

Reconciliation

The Lamb of God also reconciles. He reconciles us with one another and with God. We will explore both of these dimensions of reconciliation.

1. Reconciliation to God

Reconciliation to God is at the heart of the sacrifice of Jesus. His crucifixion is the crashing, awesome, painful, terrible collision between sinful people and our righteous creator God. Jesus crucified is our sins crashing into God.[2] In Jesus crucified, humanity spat in the face of God. We (humanity) beat him with our fists and slapped him with our hands. We shredded his back by whipping him with thongs tipped with pieces of sharp bone and lead. We nailed his hands and feet to a cross and mocked him as he died.

How does God respond? God invites us to be embraced in his forgiving love. The cross reveals how far God will go in his quest for reconciliation with us. Jesus crucified is the most remarkable and distinctive difference between the Christian faith and all other religions. Islam views God as the merciful one who sends a book of revelation to us, but God is never affected by what we do. Buddha taught that no God will help us find salvation; Buddha's hands and arms are always folded. In traditional Buddhism, the person must find salvation on his own.

Some people view God as coming with clenched fists threatening us. Others consider God to be indifferent. In dramatic contrast, the arms and hands of God in Christ are open, wounded hands. Those open hands seek us and invite us so that we might be reconciled to God.

Missionary Paul puts our reconciliation to God this way:

> Once you were alienated from God and were enemies in your minds because of your evil behavior. But now he has reconciled you by Christ's physical body through death to present you holy in his sight, without blemish and free from accusation. (Col. 1:21,22)

2. Reconciliation to others

Let's step back for a moment and look at a worldwide practice of reconciliation to others. This will help us understand Jesus as reconciler.

Sacrifice the innocent one. When I was teaching world religions at Kenyatta University College on the outskirts of Nairobi, Kenya, I asked some eighty students to write a paper entitled, "Reconciliation." They were to ask their grandparents and great grandparents how they worked for reconciliation when there was conflict in times past, before they knew anything about Christianity or Islam. entitled, "Reconciliation." They were to ask their grandparents and great grandparents how they worked for reconciliation when there was conflict in times past, before they knew anything about Christianity or Islam.

Those research papers astonished me. Reconciliation always involved the sacrifice of a perfect animal or even human. Always. Whatever the conflict: between a father and son, siblings, husband and wife, several tribes, neighbors disputing land boundaries, God and the tribe, the peace was always established by sacrificing an innocent victim. Most often those seeking reconciliation ate the sacrifice together.

About that time the French anthropologist, René Girard, began writing about his amazing discoveries about sacrifice in societies around the world. Girard's research revealed that in traditional religions everywhere, people seeking reconciliation killed an innocent victim. The sacrifice of an innocent animal or human, in the quest for reconciliation, was universal in traditional religions.[3] The African experience fit a global pattern.

Girard perceived that sacrifice is necessary for the following reason. Those who are hostile toward one another select the most perfect animal or human they can offer. The victim is always innocent of having anything to do with the hostility.

Then those who are against each other turn their hostility against the innocent victim instead of against each other. The victim dies, and does not take vengeance. The sacrificial victim has taken the violence on itself without hitting back. That breaks the cycle of violence and hostility.

Girard was amazed. He concluded that this universal practice of sacrifice for reconciliation must be pointing to a central universal truth. In recent years he has concluded that the truth center is the crucifixion of Jesus Christ. Jesus is the most excellent sacrifice humanity or God could offer.

Jesus embraces the enemy! A Croatian born theologian, Miroslav Volf, who is now teaching at Yale University in the United States, presses Girard's insights further. He points out that Jesus is not just the innocent victim who simply acquiesces to the violence in the spirit of forgiveness. Miroslav sees Jesus actively seeking the enemy so he might embrace and forgive the one who is hostile. Jesus is not passive. He pursues and persistently seeks to redeem and reconcile, to embrace and forgive all who live in hostility toward God or toward one another.[4] However, take note: the reconciliation offered by Jesus Christ is impossible unless we repent and accept his forgiveness and his embrace.

At the time of Jesus, Israel (Jewish people) and the Gentiles (the other nations) were not reconciled. Jews even refused to eat with Gentiles. Yet both Jews and Gentiles turned against Jesus to crucify him. They both hurled mean-spirited and hateful hostility against Jesus, even as he was dying. They killed the innocent one. As he died he cried out, "Father, forgive them."

The church: A reconciled people. In the following chapters we shall explore the creation of the church. I note here, however, that one of the most amazing surprises of the early church was that Jews and Gentiles were reconciled. How could that be?

Both Gentiles and Jews crucified Jesus. Neither group wanted Jesus to be their king. However, the Gentiles and Jews were not only hostile toward Jesus, they were also hostile toward one another. Jesus was crucified in a milieu of Gentile and Jewish hostility; he absorbed their hostility, and forgave. In that way he made it possible to break the cycle of hostility. Those who repented of their hostility and accepted the forgiveness and embrace of Christ, became the church; that early church was a most remarkable and surprising community of reconciliation.

One early Christian missionary, Paul, wrote about this astonishing reality in a letter to a new church. He said,

> For he himself is our peace, who has made the two one and has destroyed the barrier, the dividing wall of hostility . . . and in this one body to reconcile both of

them to God through the cross, by which he put to death their hostility. (Eph. 2:14,16)

Astonishing reconciliation in Kenya. In the early 1950s there was a civil war in Kenya, with the Mau Mau fighting for independence from British colonialism. There were Christians in Kenya who were nicknamed the people of the Lamb, because they sought to live in the costly reconciliation that Jesus offers. They would not participate in the fighting; rather they stood between the white and black people who were fighting each other. Many were martyred; in fact, in central Kenya there is a church built in remembrance of those who died as reconcilers.

Some years ago, I rode my 70 cc. Honda cycle into those hills where the Mau Mau war once ravaged the land. I met one of those people of the Lamb, Heshbon Mwangi, at his home. His face was creased with a ghastly scar from knife slashes he sustained when nearby villagers tried to kill him during that war.

I asked, "Why did you refuse to defend yourself with a gun or a knife?"

Heshbon spoke slowly, "In our traditional religion when there was hostility, we killed a reconciliation goat. We ate it together. After that we had to live in peace."

"Jesus is the Lamb of God," he continued. "At the communion table (Eucharist) we eat bread and drink wine, symbols of his reconciliation sacrifice when he was crucified. That means I can never do violence against anyone for whom Christ has given his life as a reconciliation sacrifice."

After a pause, Heshbon continued, "If in the past we sought peace through eating the sacrificial goat, how much more is reconciliation established when we have participated in the communion of the sacrifice of Jesus, the Lamb of God. Therefore, I can never be violent against another person for whom Christ has died."

Redeemed People

In John's vision recorded in Revelation 5, elders, creatures, a billion angels, and all creation sing with joy when the Lamb receives the scroll because the Lamb is able to redeem people for God from sin and death. These people are from every tribe and language and nation. These redeemed people serve God. They reign on the earth.

Angels and people sing. However, here all other creatures are also singing. Why would all creation sing with joy when the Lamb receives the scroll?

Recall when Adam and Eve turned away from God. At that time God declared that the earth will be "cursed because of you." In our selfishness we exploit the earth, wounding it rather than caring for it. We damage the soil and resources. We, also, often treat the animals cruelly.

Redeemed people don't curse the earth; they bless it and care for it. Redeemed people are gentle with the animals. The earth and all creation are blessed and rejoice when redeemed people "reign." It is, therefore, not surprising that all creatures sing with joy.

Reconciliation in Mostar

I saw an example of redeemed and reconciled people reigning on earth when I visited Bosnia in April, 1997. I and my companions traveled to the city of Mostar by bus. We saw destroyed homes in every town. Riding through some areas, every house as far as we could see had been bombed or rocketed.

When we arrived in Mostar, we saw astonishing destruction. East Mostar is Muslim; it was eighty percent destroyed. Christian West Mostar was also heavily bombed and rocketed. This destruction was especially horrible, because it was produced by neighbor against neighbor.

During the height of the Bosnian war, Nikola Skrinjaric and his fiancee, Sandra, went to Mostar for their wedding. They did this as a sign of hope in a city where there was no hope. During their honeymoon rockets destroyed houses and killed people all around them. Nevertheless, they stayed in Mostar for most of the next three years. They learned to zigzag across the streets whenever they went outside, dodging snipers, rockets, and grenades. In the name of Jesus Christ, they helped the homeless, hungry, and wounded.[5]

We worshiped with a new congregation in a rocket-damaged building in East Mostar. About forty people gathered for worship. Their background was Muslim, Croat, and Serb. I was told that nowhere else in that city were people from these different groups talking with one another, unless compelled to do so by the international forces. There was as yet no peace in Mostar, except for two churches that Nikola and Sandra had helped to plant in that city.

That night we experienced a baptism of joy. Forgiveness and reconciliation had united these former enemies in deep bonds of love for one another. I was told that people in that congregation had been involved in various ways in the hate and destruction. Now they were a redeemed people, rescued from the hate and violence that had inflamed their city and their personal lives.

Although they were a tiny community, their spirit of forgiveness, reconciliation, and joy made the whole city take note. They were a redeemed good news community in a city that yearned for some signs of hope. Jesus Christ had literally rescued them from death. They were a reconciled and redeemed people from among the peoples of Mostar. They were "reigning" in Mostar as a people serving God with joy and hope.

That is why Jesus is worthy to take the scroll of history in his hand. The One who is the Lamb of God creates what I experienced in Mostar in April, 1997. No other authority can create that kind of miracle in a context of such evil and hate. That is why the whole universe rejoices that Jesus, the Lamb of God, is entrusted with the destiny of human history.

• • •

Imagine John all alone on the Island of Patmos. He has a vision. He is peering into heaven.

In his vision he sees the most astonishing thing imaginable. A slain lamb is standing in the center of the throne of God. God gives that Lamb a sealed scroll. Then all of heaven and creation begin to sing with delight because the Lamb has that scroll.

Visions like this one have deep meaning. They are like a Picasso painting. You must reflect on the picture to fathom the meaning in the painting. That is the nature of this vision. It is a picture of reality from God's viewpoint.

There are different interpretations of this vision. Here is what I see in the vision, but, of course, you will want to reflect on what you see in the vision. As I reflect on the meaning of this vision it is so astounding that it makes me blink. I believe that scroll is human history; it is your life and my life. It is sealed. Our sinfulness is tightly sealed in that scroll.

Most certainly the Lamb is Jesus Christ, crucified and risen. The throne is the power center of history and in fact the universe. Jesus crucified and risen is in the power center of the universe; this means that Jesus crucified is the power of God. That is totally astonishing–the crucified Jesus at the power center.

God gives Jesus Christ that scroll, because he is worthy to take it. Why is he worthy? He is worthy because he is able to deal with the sin problem hidden deep in our lives, our homes, our communities, and our world.

This vision is astounding. God has entrusted to Jesus Christ, the crucified and risen King, the destiny of human history. The vision assures us that our destiny is in the worthy hands of Jesus.

Jesus is worthy because through his sacrificial crucifixion he is empowered to offer the gift of forgiveness, reconciliation, and redemption. All creation is blessed and rejoices as they see Jesus redeeming people from sin and death. Every creature throughout heaven and earth sings for joy.

10

THE POWER OF GOD

Background Scripture: Matthew 28

"What awesome power!" I gasped, when I stepped into the Apollo/Saturn V Center at the Kennedy Space Museum at Cape Canaveral, Florida. I was gazing at a Saturn V rocket similar to the one that took Neil Armstrong, Buzz Aldrin, and Michael Collins to the moon in 1969.

That rocket weighs 6.2 million pounds. It is 363 feet long. I could not imagine the power packed into that machine to hurtle 3,100 tons away from earth with a payload headed to the moon.

However, the energy packed into Saturn V is puny when compared to our nearest star, the sun. That star consumes 4,000,000 tons of mass every second in a hydrogen thermonuclear reaction that sustains heat of twenty-seven million degrees F. in its inner core. Our sun is only one of 300 billion stars in our Milky Way galaxy. There are some fifty billion other galaxies. It is trite to say it, but there is a lot of power packed into our universe.

Smash 'em Power

The source and nature of power is fundamentally significant to our well-being. In Chapter 2 we reflected on the notions of power developed in evolutionary theory. We noted that the theory of the survival of the fittest is cruel. It feeds the "might makes right" notions that have been so diabolical in the twentieth century. The dominant culture in the United States is awash with the notion that violence is the way to make things right. Theologian Walter Wink observes that Americans largely agree with the violent assumptions of the ancient Babylonian nature myths.[1] (See chapter 6.)

In those myths the earth, sky, and mankind came about through violent conflict among the gods. Order was imposed violently by victorious gods. The male divinity imposed his supremacy by killing the female goddess, and in human society, likewise, man was expected to impose his rule over woman. Violence was the essence of humankind, for we were formed from the blood of a god dying in violent combat.

Violence was also a theme in the ancient Egyptian myths. Egypt was formed and sustained by the incest and violence of the gods. North American culture is far more attuned to those violent myths than to the nonviolence of the creation account in Genesis.[2]

In the United States it is assumed that power must exercise violence to bring order out of chaos. The good is established and preserved through violence. Even the cartoons for children too often communicate that message. The way to deal with bad people is for good people to bash them. That is the message of Batman. Bash 'em; smash 'em.

Violence preserves freedoms for United States' citizens. Violence and the threat of violence is required to assure the good way of life. The survival of the fittest requires the destruction of those not fit. That is a significant theme in the American story; it begins with the destruction of indigenous peoples and cultures, the American Indians.

The Word of Power

In dramatic contrast, the creation of the world described in the Bible is nonviolent (see chapter 2). God speaks, and the earth is created. There is no hint of chaotic turmoil, gods gouging out the entrails of enemy gods, or violence. God speaks, creating a good earth with all the creatures therein and entrusts the development and care of this wonderful creation to humans. God's Word is all powerful. The Word is God's creative self expression. He speaks and creation happens.

Power incarnated

Remarkably, Jesus Christ is the Word of God in human form. That is one of the meanings of the name, Son of God, that we noted in the last chapter.

John writes that

> In the beginning was the Word, and the Word was with God, and the Word was God. He was with God in the beginning. . . .
> The Word became flesh and made his dwelling among us. We have seen his glory, the glory of the One and Only who came from the Father, full of grace and truth. (John 1:1-14)

If the Christian faith were a philosophy or speculation, it should be dismissed as lunacy; the claims are so outrageous. A carpenter from Nazareth is the incarnation of the power and authority that created the universe. Any person who wanted to develop a credible religion certainly would not come up with such an off-the-wall notion. No other faith, religion, or ideology has ever imagined anything so ludicrous.

The New Testament apostolic writers, however, were persistent. They had been with Jesus. They believed that he was indeed the fullness of the presence and power of God in human form. They were convinced that there was no other satisfactory explanation for the authority and power that Jesus so surprisingly demonstrated.

One of the New Testament writers exclaims, "The Son is the radiance of God's glory and the exact representation of his being, sustaining all things by his powerful word" (Heb. 1:3). Elsewhere we read,

That which was from the beginning, which we have heard, which we have seen with our eyes, which we have looked at and our hands have touched—this we proclaim concerning the Word of life. The life appeared; we have seen it and testify to it, and we proclaim to you the eternal life, which was with the Father and has appeared to us. (1 John 1:1-2)

Vulnerable Power

The vulnerability of God is the greatest surprise of the Christian faith. The abiding astonishment of the gospel is that God, who created the fifty billion galaxies in space, became Immanuel, God with Us, in the delicate embryo in Mary's womb. The Word that created and sustains the universe with mighty power was that baby in a manger in Bethlehem, the refugee child fleeing to Egypt.

Then there is the cross. The One on that cross is not only King of the Jews, as the inscription announced above his head. He is also the Son of God, Immanuel, the Word of God in human form. The Word of Power through whom the universe was created suffers and dies at the hands of the very people he had created and whom he loves. Here we meet the ultimate distinctiveness of the Christian faith when measured against all other religions or ideologies. Swiss theologian Hans Kung writes,

> The cross then is not only example and model, but ground, strength and norm of the Christian faith: the great distinctive reality which distinguishes this faith and its Lord in the world market from the religious and irreligious ideologies, from other competing religions and utopias and their Lords, and plunges its roots at the same time into the reality of concrete life with its conflicts.[3]

The biblical writer Paul says it this way:

For the message of the cross is foolishness to those who are perishing, but to us who are being saved, it is the power of God. . . . Jews demand miraculous signs and Greeks look for wisdom, but we preach Christ crucified: a stumbling block to Jews and foolishness to Gentiles, but to those whom God has called, both Jews and Greeks, Christ the power of God and the wisdom of God. For the foolishness of God is wiser than man's wisdom, and the weakness of God is stronger than man's strength. (1 Cor. 1:18, 22-25)

The Slain Lamb Stands

Recall that John exclaimed, "Then I saw a Lamb, looking as if it had been slain, standing in the center of the throne. . . " (Rev. 5:6). That Lamb is a metaphor for Jesus crucified and risen. The Lamb slain, "stands." He stands in the center of the throne of God. He is alive. He takes the scroll. John's vision is an affirmation that Jesus Christ rose from the dead.

Eye witness reports of the resurrection of Jesus are recorded in the concluding portions of each of the four Gospel accounts of his life and teachings. After his death on the cross, his associates placed him in a tomb, a cave in a rock. They placed a stone in front of the cave entrance, and the authorities sealed the tomb so no one could steal the body of Jesus. They placed guards at the tomb.

Matthew describes what happened in this way:

After the Sabbath, at dawn on the first day of the week, Mary Magdalene and the other Mary went to look at the tomb. There was a violent earthquake, for an angel of the Lord came down from heaven and, going to the tomb, rolled back the stone and sat on it. . . The guards were so afraid of him that they shook and became like dead men.

The angel said to the women, "Do not be afraid, for I know that you are looking for Jesus, who was crucified. He is not here; he has risen, just as he said. Come and see the place where he lay." (Matt. 28:1-2, 4-6)

For the next forty days, Jesus appeared occasionally to his followers. He had a glorified body; he could appear and disappear and go through walls. Yet he was not a ghost. He moved about as a total, real person. He ate. He conversed. His hands showed the scars of the nails from his crucifixion. He really was Jesus (Luke 24:13-42; John 20:19-21:15).

In John's vision of the Lamb in the center of the throne of God, that Lamb looks like it had been slain, yet it also stands. That is a metaphor of Jesus crucified and risen. The hands of the One who takes the scroll are scarred by nail prints.

The resurrection of Jesus from the dead is the guarantee that he is indeed the eternal King who God promised to King David a thousand years earlier. It is the confirmation that Jesus is the Son of God. The resurrection is the assurance that Jesus is the revelation in history of the Word of Power through whom the universe is created and sustained. The resurrection is the confirmation that Jesus is Lord; that is the universal confession of all Christians.

The Mystery of the Cross

There is mystery about Jesus crucified and risen as the power of God. Theologions use the term "atonement" to try to capture what happened. In the previous chapter we explored the several dimensions of this mystery: forgiveness, reconciliation, and redemption. In the next pages we shall explore other dimensions of the mystery of the atoning death and resurrection of Jesus Christ.

Some dismiss the atonement as nonsense, for if they cannot explain the mystery, they choose to ignore it. C. S. Lewis wryly observes that we do not do this in other arenas of life, like eating.[4] I have just enjoyed lunch. I know that lunch is empowering me to think and write. Yet the scientific community does not yet fully understand all that has transpired in converting my peanut butter and honey sandwich into energy to write. Nevertheless, just because I do not understand the mystery of food empowering my brain with energy, I will not be deterred from eating.

Indeed, as we explore the mystery of the crucifixion and resurrection of Jesus, we do so in awareness that even eternity will not be enough time to fathom its wonders. Nevertheless, we shall explore six surprising expressions of that wonder.

The first surprise: Jesus crucified and risen reveals nonviolent redemptive love in confronting evil. Jesus will strike the nations with his sword. We are shocked reading this in the last book of the Bible (Rev. 1:16; 2:12; 2:16; 19:15; 19:21). Is this the same Jesus who, when he was crucified, extended forgiveness for those who had done this great wrong against him? Is this the same Jesus who rebuked a follower for trying to defend him with a sword the night of his arrest just before his crucifixion? Is this the Jesus whose only weapon, when chasing the merchants from the temple, was a fragile whip of cords that he used to get the cattle moving? Jesus as a sword-bearing warrior slaughtering his enemies in Revelation doesn't seem to be consistent with Jesus of the Gospels. However, we discover that "Out of his *mouth* comes a sharp sword with which to strike down the nations" (Rev. 19:15).

Indeed Revelation describes colossal conflict between Christ and the forces of evil. We are assured that Jesus Christ will triumph. He wields the sword of victory, but it is always the sword from his mouth. What is this sword from the mouth of Jesus that strikes the nations? It is the truth. Jesus triumphs through declaring and exercising the truth. Even in the final drama of history, Jesus does not smash and bash those who reject him. He wins the battle with the weapon of truth.

Jesus is committed to the truth; his followers should likewise confront evil with truth. Commitment to truth is not neutral or inactive. Truth confronts. Truth is expressed in witness, testimony, persuasion, boldness, patience, love, and power.

One who embraces the truth of Christ is confident in the power of the gospel, and seeks to confront strongholds that oppose the gospel through bold and confident witness. Disciples of Jesus are commissioned to practice the truth of the gospel in what they do and what they say. Truth is anchored in love, bold and confident love that is prepared to suffer for the truth (John 1:1-18; Acts 1:8; 28:23).

What is this truth that will prevail? The Power Center of the universe is Jesus Christ crucified and risen. That is ultimate truth and power.

When living in Somalia, I walked to the town tea shop one evening with students. As we sipped generously sweet tea spiced with "garful" and "heil," these Muslim student friends began talking about how impractical the Christian faith is in comparison to Islam. They expounded, "You have told us that Jesus taught that people should forgive their enemies. That is not practical. Islam is practical. As Muslims we strike our enemy in a way that teaches him to respect us."

I countered, "However, when you hit back, your enemy will crouch in the bushes sometime, and get you. So the cycle of revenge never stops. Jesus offers another way. Forgive. Show kindness to your enemy. Even die at his hands. That is the only way to stop the cycle of revenge. If you don't hit back, the cycle stops."

In recent years these wonderful beloved Somali people have experienced self destruction as the cycle of revenge between clans goes on and on. Somalia as a whole is a society that has never known the invitation of Jesus to another way.

About the same time I was having that tea shop conversation in Somalia, Kenya to our south was on the brink of intertribal civil war because of a political assassination. In the midst of that crisis, some 10,000 Christians from tribes across the nation met in the central highlands. They proclaimed for all to hear that they were a reconciled people from the very tribes teetering toward conflict. They announced that come what may, they would never kill one another.

Jesus said, "A new command I give you: Love one another. As I have loved you, so you must love one another" (John 13:34). Elsewhere Jesus says, "Love your enemies. . . " Matt. 5:44). The cross reveals what Jesus meant by this new command. The love revealed on the cross is the foundation of all Christian ethics. There is nothing cowardly, weak, or impotent about that kind of love. Love-based ethics are power.

The second surprise: Jesus crucified and risen breaks the powers of the nature gods. Recall that Adam and Eve turned to the tree of the knowledge of good and evil for fruit to make them wise (chapter 3). They looked to that tree rather than God for their authority. They looked to nature for their authority.

From the beginning of human history, people have invited nature and its gods to usurp the authority of God. In earlier chapters we have observed the significance of the divinities of nature among peoples around the world.

Jesus was crucified on a tree on a hill; both tree and hill are universal symbols of nature worship. The biblical Scriptures say that anyone who hangs on a tree is cursed (Deut. 21:23). As noted before, behind the smiling face of the nature gods, there are leopard's teeth. Even tree and hill are not benign when they usurp the place of God as our focus of worship and authority.

Jesus is nailed to the wood of a tree. In his death on that tree on a hill, Jesus exposes the violent cruelty of the divinized powers of nature. In his resurrection, he breaks those powers. The so-called natural law of the survival of the fittest is also broken; no more shall the laws of nature have the last word.

This is astonishing good news for all who are ensnared by the powers of nature, whether those powers be secularized natural law, or the worship of nature gods.

Listen to the comments of a K'ekchi' pastor from Alta Verapaz in the central highlands of Guatemala. "In what ways is

Jesus Christ good news for these people?" I mused as I joined in an evening of worship that convened in the pastor's living room.

In his message that night the pastor asserted, "Christ frees us from the fear of owls that hoot at night and black animals that scoot across our path. God created the owl and the black animals; they are not omens of the nature gods. Live in the freedom that Christ provides!"

Nature can also ensnare us even when not worshiped as a divinity. Our modern exaggerated trust in technology can become a cross that demeans both nature and humankind. Witness Chernobyl in the Ukraine that spewed lethal radiation throughout vast regions of Central Europe when its atomic reactors went berserk (1996), or the atomic accident at Three Mile Island in Middletown, Pennsylvania (1979).

Jesus crucified on nature's cross exposes demeaning ways in which we use nature. Yet he triumphs over the cross, thereby revealing a new life-sustaining way of relating to creation.

The third surprise: Jesus crucified and risen unmasks the powers of evil and triumphs over them. The biblical Scriptures proclaim, "And having disarmed the powers and authorities, he made a public spectacle of them, triumphing over them by the cross" (Col. 2:15).

These powers are both demonic and human. Why did the powers gang up against Jesus? He healed the sick. He raised the dead to life. He forgave sins. He cast out demons. He fed the hungry. He blessed children. He respected and empowered women. He taught righteous living. He loved and redeemed sinful people. He confronted injustice. He welcomed strangers. He loved and obeyed God. He opposed religion that was bereft of compassion. He was all that we know in our souls to be right and true. Yet the powers crucified Jesus: religious, political, economic, demonic, personal, and the power of crowds.

The cross exposes how evil the powers are. The cross makes a "public spectacle of them." But that is not all there is to it.

Jesus' resurrection has broken the might of the powers, including Satan's power.

During the 1980s Ethiopia suffered under a Marxist government. It was cruel and ruthless. Even high school students who were considered counter-revolutionary were shot. Occasionally the body of a dead child was thrown in the parents' yard, but the family had to pay for the cost of the bullets used to kill the child before they could redeem the body for burial.

In that context a university teacher, Fekru Zeleke, was arrested, beaten, and placed in prison. His crime: he was sharing the message of Jesus Christ with interested university students. He was a member of the Meserete Kristos Church that had been declared illegal by the government. He had been assigned to a university far from home, family, and friends.

The chief police officer confronted Fekru and with a pistol in his hand said in great anger, "You have no authority to speak of Jesus Christ to anyone. Your church is illegal."

Although a pistol was pointing at him, Fekru responded, "I do have authority to speak of Jesus Christ. Jesus has risen from the dead and has triumphed over all authorities. In his authority I shall continue to witness."

The angry officer exploded, "We can kill you for that."

"That is no problem to me." Fekru replied. "Jesus has triumphed over death."

Today that government in Ethiopia is no more. Jesus is being heard and believed across the land. In fact, the officer who apprehended Fekru was put in prison, and Fekru visited him and expressed compassion to him in his distress.

The powers thought they had killed goodness when they crucified Jesus. They thought they had gotten the upper hand, and could continue undisturbed in their independent and self-centered ways. It is not so.

Jesus has broken the authority of the powers. He has shamed them publicly by revealing the extent that they will go to reject goodness. He has triumphed over them in his resurrection. Jesus who stands in the center of the throne of God has ultimate power and authority, not the powers that oppose his rule.

The fourth surprise: Jesus crucified and risen frees us from the shackles of religion. Religions everywhere are inclined to enslave people.

In the Jean-Jacques Annaud film, *Seven Years in Tibet*, Buddhist devotees crawl on hands, knees, and stomachs many miles across the highlands in pilgrimage to the holy shrine in Lhasa. Annaud captures authentic insight into the tremendous religious devotion of these Tibetan Buddhists. Religion can become an awesome burden.

At the time of Jesus, the Jewish religious system had developed multitudes of regulations that people should follow to please God. For example, one could walk only a certain distance from home on the Sabbath, because the Ten Commandments required that a person rest on the Sabbath.

In Nairobi we lived across the street from a Muslim mosque. Every morning when one could tell a black thread from a white thread (about 4:30 a.m.), the imam would call people to come for prayer with the loudspeaker affixed to the minaret. The faithful went through ablutions and the prayer ritual at that time. In fact, they were called to prayer five times a day, and went through a total of seventeen prayer cycles each day. Each prayer cycle included the Arabic recitation of the opening chapter of the Quran.

In contrast to such religious practices, Jesus lived in freedom. He respected religious practices, but was not enslaved by them. For example, he healed people on the Sabbath, even in the worship time in the synagogue. It was his collision with Jewish religious belief and practice that as much as anything led to the conspiracy to kill him.

Religious laws and beliefs were marshaled in the case against Jesus, and used as justification to kill him. Religious law cursed Jesus with its heavy burdens. He bore that curse, but triumphed over it in his resurrection. The Scriptures say, "Christ redeemed us from the curse of the law by becoming a curse for us. . . " (Gal. 3:13).

When we were living in Somalia, a number of Muslims were becoming believers in Jesus Christ. I noticed that none of the believers knelt or bowed their heads to the floor in prayer, ever. That surprised me, for kneeling in prayer with the face to the floor is the way Muslims pray. I thought that practice might continue in the church. So I asked why they now stood in prayer.

"Oh, don't you understand!" one of their leaders exclaimed. "In Islam we were slaves of God and submitted to religious rituals. No more! Jesus has freed us. We are now sons and daughters of God. Sons and daughters always stand and converse with their Father, they do not kneel with faces to the ground."

The Scriptures say,

> But when the time had fully come, God sent his Son, born of a woman, born under law (religion) to redeem those under law, that we might receive the full rights of sons. Because you are sons, God sent the Spirit of his Son into our hearts, the Spirit who calls out, 'Abba, Father.' So you are no longer a slave, but a son; and since you are a son, God has made you also an heir. (Gal. 4:4-7)

Jesus saves us from religion and introduces us into the family of God. We enjoy learning to know God as our Papa.

The fifth surprise: Jesus crucified and risen breaks the power of sin. The Scriptures say, "For we know that our old self was crucified with him so that the body of sin might be done away with, that we should no longer be slaves to sin" (Rom. 6:6). Elsewhere we read, "But now he has appeared once for all at the end of the ages to do away with sin by the sacrifice of himself" (Heb. 9:26).

Jesus Christ frees those who believe from the bondage to sin. The Scriptures promise, "For sin shall not be your master, because you are not under law, but under grace" (Rom. 6:14). Jesus called this transformation, "born again" (John 3:3).

Menno Simons' view was that

> they are the true congregation of Christ who are truly converted, who are born from above of God, who are of a regenerate mind by the operation of the Holy Spirit through the hearing of the divine Word, and have become children of God, have entered into obedience to him, and live unblameably in his holy commandment, and according to his holy will with all their days, or from the moment of their call.[5]

Robert is from the opposite side of the world from our home in the United States; he comes from one of Asia's robust nations. As a guest, he joined us for supper one evening. His story: he was a womanizer, an alcoholic, a violent man, once imprisoned for murder. Today he is a righteous man, gracious and gentle, a man devoted to his wife, a man of integrity and deep love for others. Why the transformation?

Robert says it simply: "Jesus died for my sins; now I am free."

Everyone needs a similar transformation. Not all of us have killed another person or subdued another sexually, but all of us have sinned. Jesus says that impure sexual thoughts or resentful anger is sin. So is self-righteous self-sufficiency. So is not sharing our wealth or desiring the wealth of another person. In the light of Jesus, we all discover that we need salvation from sin.

The sixth surprise: Jesus crucified and risen frees us from death. Shortly before his crucifixion, Jesus promised, "I am the resurrection and the life. He who believes in me will live, even though he dies" (John 11:25). Later he added, "I go to prepare a place for you, I will come back and take you to be with me that you also may be where I am" (John 14:3).

A hope for some form of life after death is universal. Religions speak to that hope. However, in the resurrection promise of Jesus, we meet an astonishing distinction of the Christian faith: bodily resurrection. Just as Jesus rose from the dead bodily, we shall also rise someday at the grand climax of history.

The notion of a bodily resurrection does not arise out of the wishful thinking of some fringe philosophers or religious speculators. It is too idealistic and wild a notion to have gained credibility in any such manner. It is rather a response to the very real event of the resurrection of Jesus Christ. There are credible witnesses to his resurrection.

This Jesus promised that we will also be raised from the dead. The belief in the bodily resurrection of the dead is, therefore, based on the *event* of the resurrection of Jesus and his *promise* that those who believe in him will likewise rise to be with him eternally.

In my childhood in East Africa, I would always know when someone died. Hysterical weeping arose. However, as soon as Jesus was received by a family, the hopeless death wails changed dramatically in the homes of Christians. Peace and hope is the best way to describe the death of Christians. These funerals among a people who had only recently learned of Christ were characterized by songs of praise and confident hope.

A million years from now we will still be young. Jesus has conquered death for all who believe in him. What an astonishing hope.

• • •

Power!

How is it possible that a Jewish rabbi from Nazareth wounded, despised, and crucified is the power of God who triumphs over death and all evil powers? That is astounding.

A missionary of the early church, Paul, wrote about this astonishment to the Ephesians, a church that consisted of people from incredibly different backgrounds, both devout Jews who had embraced the laws and beliefs of Judaism, and worshipers of the fertility nature goddess, Diana. The Lamb slain who stands in the throne of God had created a community of redeemed people in Ephesus.

With delight and thankfulness Paul wrote,

> I pray also that the eyes of your heart may be enlightened in order that you may know the hope to which he has called you, the riches of his glorious inheritance in the saints, and his incomparably great power for us who believe. That power is like the working of his mighty strength, which he exerted in Christ when he raised him from the dead and seated him at his right hand in the heavenly realms, far above all rule and authority, power and dominion, and every title that can be given, not only in the present age but also in the one to come. And God placed all things under his feet and appointed him to be the head over everything for the church which is his body, the fullness of him who fills everything in every way. (Eph. 1:18-23)

The next chapter entitled, "The Coach and the Team" will explore the meaning of the church that Paul refers to in these verses.

11

THE COACH AND THE TEAM

Background Scripture: Acts 1:1-11; 2:1-47

Salvation from poverty through basketball. In cold, rain, or heat, the Chicago youth portrayed in the documentary film, *Hoop Dreams*, throw the basketball through the hoop with astonishing commitment.

These urban youth believed that noteworthy achievement in basketball was their only hope of breaking out of poverty. Day after day, with tenacious endurance, these elementary and high school youth practiced basketball. They hoped to join a college basketball team someday.

However, accomplishment on the torrid asphalt courts of Chicago's south side was not enough. A college basketball coach had to invite them onto his team. That was the only way out. A coach had to intervene and help them.

The Coach

Jesus promised to send his followers a coach. *Paracleitos* is the Greek term used in the Scriptures for the Coach that Jesus promised. (The New Testament was first written in Greek.) In the Greek language a paracleitos is the advocate who helps a person when facing accusations in a court. English Bibles usually translate the term as Helper or Counselor.

The promised Coach or Helper would invite people to join the team that Jesus captained. The Helper would empower the followers of Jesus in their confrontation with sin and evil in the courts of life. He would be the Coach who would lead their team to victory, analogous to the coach who redeemed youth from the asphalt jungles portrayed in the film, *Hoop Dreams*, and who led the team to triumph.

The coming of the Counselor was a significant part of the conversation at the Passover meal the evening before Jesus was arrested. Jesus told his followers that night that crucifixion awaited him. He was concerned for their well being. He yearned that they as a team persevere and triumph over sin and evil.

The spirit of truth!

It was in that context of concern for the team that Jesus promised that God would send the Counselor after his crucifixion. The Counselor would be "the Spirit of truth" (John 14:16,17). He was the Holy Spirit who would teach "all things" (John 14:26).

Jesus promised that the Counselor, "will convict the world of guilt in regard to sin and righteousness and judgment. . . . He will bring glory to me by taking from what is mine and making it known to you" (John 16:8, 14) .

College students often ask, "How does God call?"

There are many ways that God prepares us to hear his call, such as circumstances or the witness concerning Jesus Christ that a friend shares with us. However, it is the Holy Spirit who plants in our soul the surprising inner conviction that we are invited to join the team that Jesus captains. The inner urging that we should believe in Jesus Christ and sign up with his team is always the work of the Holy Spirit.

It is conviction!

In an upstairs room on Waterloo Road in Hong Kong one night, we witnessed the presence of the Holy Spirit. A group of Christian taxi cab drivers met for Bible study and prayer. One had brought a friend who had never been to church before. He was a big man with a hard looking face. He was addicted to gambling. As we sang, the hard look on his tough face became more gentle, andhe began to sob quite loudly. He was terribly embarrassed to be crying in our presence.

However, his friend whispered, "That is alright. It is conviction. The Holy Spirit is convicting you. After the worship we will help you understand. People often cry when convicted."

It is the Holy Spirit who convicts. He reveals to us that we are sinful and that we need salvation; it is the Holy Spirit who reveals that Jesus is the Savior who has come to rescue; it is the Holy Spirit who calls us to believe in Jesus Christ; it is the Holy Spirit who empowers us to walk in the Christian Way; it is the Holy Spirit who creates and forms and coaches the team that Jesus captains.

Born again!

Not one of us on our own is capable of such transformations; these transformations are the work of the Holy Spirit. In fact Jesus called this re-creation of the person "born again."

That is what utterly surprised a respected religious leader, Nicodemus. He came to visit Jesus secretly at night. Jesus declared, "I tell you the truth, no one can see the kingdom of God unless he is born again" (John 3:3). Nicodemus was astounded. Jesus explained that this is the work of the Spirit of God.

Baptism is a sign of the work of the Holy Spirit. Churches such as Orthodox, Catholic, or Lutheran will baptize the babies of believing parents. This is a sign that the Holy Spirit is working, even in the little baby. All such churches have a confirmation celebration when the child is old enough to declare her faith and commitment to Christ.

Other churches such as Baptist, Mennonite, or Pentecostal will baptize only adults, or persons old enough to make a public confession of faith in Christ. They see baptism as a public witness that people have heard and obeyed the Holy Spirit; they have repented of their sins, believe in Jesus Christ, and the Holy Spirit has begun a new creation in them. They are "born again."

Conversion is another name for being born again. When people repent their sins, receive the forgiveness Jesus offers, and commits their lives to Jesus, they are converted. They have turned around; they are now following Jesus. The Holy Spirit is who enables and empowers conversion or the new birth. In fact, one of the great mysteries of the Christian Way is that the Holy Spirit lives in the converted person.

Jesus promised that the Holy Spirit would be a Comforter. He comforts from within the person. The Holy Spirit in the converted person also nurtures precious fruit: "love, joy, peace, patience, kindness, goodness, faithfulness, gentleness, and self-control" (Gal. 5:22,23). The Holy Spirit is our astonishing coach. He calls us to join the team; he teaches, forms, and leads the team into victory.

Jesus' Astonishing Ascension

Forty days after Jesus' resurrection, he had a last meeting with his disciples. We are not sure how often Jesus appeared to them after resurrection, but this was likely the eleventh time. He and his disciples were gathered near the village of Bethany, a short walk from Jerusalem. Just as on the night of his crucifixion, the Holy Spirit was very much on Jesus' mind.

Jesus promised that "you will receive power when the Holy Spirit comes on you; and you will be my witnesses in Jerusalem, and in all Judea and Samaria, and to the ends of the earth" (Acts 1:8). Then Jesus lifted his hands in blessing on the team gathered around him. As he blessed them, they were astonished.

He began to ascend into the sky until a cloud hid him from their view (Luke 24:50-53; Acts 1:9). The startled disciples stood gazing into heaven. They had never seen anything like it, a man ascending into the sky!

Mohammed and Buddha

This event, known as the ascension, is another astonishing surprise of the Christian faith. Contrasting the ascension of

Jesus with Mohammed or Buddha will reveal the significance of the event; both of these other men also founded missionary movements.

By the time Buddha died (c.483 B.C.), he had established monastic orders, educational plans, missionary strategy, scriptural teachings, and a doctrinal system.

By the time Mohammed died (A.D. 632), he had established a political order, a state constitution, an army, doctrine, religious ritual, a system of finances and care for the poor, a creed, the beginnings of recording the Muslim Scriptures, and a sacred place (ka'ba in Mecca).

What will happen next?

However, when Jesus ascended to heaven he left nothing behind to carry on the movement except a tiny cluster of perplexed disciples, who were quite capable of squabbling with each other.

Jesus left no organized set of doctrines. He had not developed a systematic theology. He left no well-organized system of teaching or instructions. He left no sacred things or places. He had established no religion or organization. There was no procedure in place to carry his movement forward. He provided no clear overall plan. He had not established a leadership pattern. His closest followers were a motley group noted for their lack of education.

Jesus had acquired no support, but rather hostility, from political or religious institutions. He left no system or plan for finances; in fact Judas who had cared for the finances of the little group had betrayed Jesus and then committed suicide. Jesus left no sacred relics behind, not even a sandal or toenail. He left no shrines or places to go to for holy pilgrimages. He left no temples or places for worship.

Jesus left no instructions on worship rituals or practices, except the command to baptize believers and to remember his death occasionally by eating bread and sharing a cup of drink together. He also washed his disciples feet, and encouraged them to do likewise. He left no creed. He left no written Scriptures like other prophets such as Moses or Jeremiah had done. Jesus left only a few bewildered disciples standing alone on the outskirts of the village of Bethany.

Our exploration of the Christian Way has reveled in the surprises along the journey. Undergirding the whole drama has been the promise of the King who would establish an eternal kingdom that would extend to the ends of the earth. Recall that Israel was called by God to be a light to the nations, and they were the people through whom the King would come. In fact, the king would sit on David's throne.

The previous four chapters here have described Jesus as that promised King and Savior. Now he had gone, leaving a few tepid disciples standing alone on a rocky field between Bethany and Jerusalem. What a colossal miscalculation it must have seemed to have been. Jesus had done nothing, as far as the disciples could see, to establish any kingdom in Israel, or anywhere else for that matter.

This will happen next!

Nevertheless, Jesus gave his disciples a word of counsel, a command, a promise, and a vision in those moments just before his departure.

The counsel: God, not the disciples, will bring about the kingdom.

The command: Wait in Jerusalem.

The promise: I will send the Holy Spirit.

The vision: You will be my witnesses to the ends of the earth (Acts 1:4-8).

The Birthday of the Church

The disciples obeyed that command to wait in Jerusalem. One hundred twenty women and men gathered there. They prayed, fasted, and waited. Day by day they waited; then on the tenth day the Counselor whom Jesus had promised came. That day was the Jewish Pentecost Feast, also known as the Feast of Harvest, when the first spring fruit and vegetables were just ripening.

The Holy Spirit appeared like tongues of fire on their heads. The place was shaken. A sound like a great wind swept over them. They began to praise God with great joy and power. People from throughout Jerusalem ran to where the disciples were gathered (Acts 2:1-4). Miraculously people were able to hear the disciples praising God, each in his native tongue.

Utterly amazed, they asked,

> "Are not all these men who are speaking Galileans? Then how is it that each of us hears them in his own native language? Parthians, Medes and Elamites; residents of Mesopotamia, Judea and Cappadocia, Pontus and Asia, Phrygia and Pamphylia, Egypt and the parts of Libya near Cyrene; visitors from Rome (both Jews and converts to Judaism); Cretans and Arabs—we hear them declaring the wonders of God in our own tongues!"

Amazed and perplexed, they asked one another, 'What does this mean?" (Acts 2:7-12).

Peter's first sermon

Peter, one of the disciples, stepped forward and preached the first Christian sermon after the death and resurrection of Jesus. Imagine the astonishment of the disciples. About two months earlier, Peter had denied that he knew anything about Jesus. That was the night Jesus was arrested and put on trial. In a most cowardly way, Peter had denied knowing Jesus, not once, but three times (John 18:15-18, 25-27).

Now Peter was transformed. The Holy Spirit had changed him. Boldly he quoted from the Scriptures written by the former prophet, Joel, and the Psalms of King David. He proclaimed that Jesus crucified and risen was the Messiah whom

God had promised to Israel through these and other prophets. He called on the people to believe in Jesus and be baptized. He pled with them to repent and turn from their sins. That day about 3,000 people believed and were baptized (Acts 2:14-41).

The church and Israel

This was the beginning of the church. For many centuries Israel had indeed been a light to the nations, God's covenant people. However, Peter quoted from the prophet Joel in his sermon where God had promised, "I will pour out my Spirit on all people. . . . And everyone who calls on the name of the Lord will be saved" (Acts 2:17, 21).

The day was now at hand when God would begin to gather "all people" into his kingdom. That is the mission of the church, a fellowship of and for all people. Israel had prepared the way; Peter's sermon proclaimed that now God's plan was that people from all nations join in God's kingdom movement throughout the whole world.

That Feast of Harvest was the birthday of the church. How appropriate that is. The first ingathering of people into the church was when the people of Israel were celebrating the first fruits of their yearly harvest. However, on that Feast of Harvest, the Holy Spirit was not gathering grapes; he was harvesting people, bringing them into the kingdom of God.

The Team

The church might be compared to the basketball teams in *Hoop Dreams*. It is the team of men and women who are playing the game of life under the authority of the Captain, Jesus. Their coach is the Holy Spirit, who has invited them onto Jesus' team and who helps them to become good players.

Ekklesia is the Greek word the New Testament uses to describe the team of Jesus' followers. In the English New Testament ekklesia is translated "church." Ekklesia means an assembly of people called to gather for a specific reason. The assembly was called for a purpose, like a village gathering together to decide on which day to have their farmer's market. Ekklesia is not a building. Neither is it a religion. It is an assembly who meet for a purpose; it is analogous to a basketball team that meets, plans, and plays together.

The first Christians used the word ekklesia from their cultural and social practices to refer to the gathering together of people in the name of Jesus.

Before his crucifixion Jesus promised,

> Again, I tell you that if two of you on earth agree about anything you ask for, it will be done for you by my Father in heaven. For where two or three come together in my name, there am I with them (Matt. 18:19-20).

That gathering together in the name of Jesus is the Christian *ekklesia* (church). Jesus is present whenever the church gathers in his name; he is present through the Holy Spirit, the Helper whom Jesus promised to send. When two or three or more meet together in Jesus' name, they are the local church. The church gathers in Jesus' name then scatters again as the members go about their normal duties.

However, the activities of the scattered church are expressed in a manner that is consistent with their primary vocation, and that is to follow and glorify Jesus Christ. Consider again the analogy of a basketball team. Every team member in *Hoop Dreams* had to take his vocation as a player in the team seriously. The life style off the court had to be consistent with a serious commitment to winning games of basketball. Likewise, the members of the church are expected to obey their Captain, Jesus, whether they are gathered in worship or scattered for work and living in their community.

Surprising Characteristics of the Church

During the twentieth century, the church has become global. Several million local churches gather in their different locations every week; all these local gatherings comprise the universal global church.

There is exhilarating diversity in the worship styles of different Christian assemblies. There are also different understandings on ways to describe the church.

Catholics emphasize the conviction that the church is where the sacraments such as the Eucharist are rightly given.

Lutherans emphasize that the church is where the gospel is rightly preached.

The Reformed churches are inclined to believe that the church is where doctrine is rightly taught and believed.

The Eastern Orthodox churches cherish a church where the mystery is reverently celebrated.

The Anabaptists believe that the church is wherever two or three meet together in Jesus' name. They cherish the promise of Jesus that "where two or three come together in my name, there am I with them" (Matt. 18:20).

In all such diversity similar worship activities are present in most Christian assemblies. There are exceptions to what I shall mention, such as the Quakers who might meet in complete silence.

When Christians gather for worship most assemblies will sing. They offer prayers of praise, confession, and requests. They hear the reading of the Scriptures and preaching. Occasionally the assembly will break bread and share a cup of juice or wine remembering Jesus' last supper before his crucifixion. This is the Eucharist or communion commemorating Jesus' sacrificial death for our sins and the new covenant relationship we experience with God. Some churches such as the Catholic or Orthodox have the Eucharist whenever the congregation gathers for worship; others have the Eucharist only occasionally.

Assemblies often include announcements concerning the well being of members or the life and ministry of the assembly. Fellowship and conversation is an important aspect of worship for churches such as the Baptists, Mennonites, Christian and

Missionary Alliance, or Pentecostals. In such congregations, at the conclusion of the benedictory prayer, conversation begins throughout the congregation as members greet one another and converse together in jovial cadences. Many such congregations plan frequent meals together that encourage fellowship and joviality together.

We shall now explore eight surprising qualities of the assembly (church) that meets in Jesus' name.

The first surprise: The church usually experiences growth. We recognize that growth does not always characterize the church. Nevertheless, during its 2,000-year history, the church globally has grown from a cluster of a few dozen disciples of Jesus at the time of his crucifixion and resurrection to a global movement of some two billion professing Christians today.

The growth began at the birthday of the church. Probably not more than a dozen people gathered around Jesus near Bethany when he ascended to heaven. Nevertheless, in ten days his disciples had baptized 3,000 people in Jerusalem. That city was the crossroads of the world, the meeting place for Asians, Africans, and Europeans. Those who were baptized came from numerous nations, and they carried the good news back to their homelands.

Biblical accounts and traditions from other sources describe the spread of the church during the lifetime of those disciples who saw Jesus ascend. These countries included today's Egypt, India, Syria, Mesopotamia, Sudan, Ethiopia, Lybia, Arabia, Turkey, the Balkans, Italy, and Spain.

Less than two centuries after the church was born, Bardaisan of Edessa in Mesopotamia exclaimed, "And what shall we say of the new race of us Christians whom Christ at His coming planted in every country and in every region?"[1]

At the time Bardaisan wrote, assemblies of Christians were scattered from India to Spain and across north Africa. During the next several centuries missionaries from Bardaisan's home country of Edessa had carried the good news of Jesus Christ to

China; others were carrying the good news far up the Nile into Sudan and into the heartland of Ethiopia, while still others were starting Christian assemblies far into eastern and western Europe.[2]

It is noteworthy that, for much of the first three centuries after Christ, the spread of Christian assemblies happened in a context of persecution. This has been true throughout the history of the church, including the twentieth century. I will comment more on the suffering of the church in the next section.

During the twentieth century the global church grew with zest. At the beginning of the century there were about 558 million professing Christians. At the close of the century the number had grown to over two billion. Thus, during the twentieth century the number of Christians increased by nearly 1.5 billion. About a third of the people on earth are now professing Christians.[3]

Much of the growth in the past century has been among the hitherto non-Christianized societies of Asia and Africa. By the end of the twentieth century two-thirds of the world's Christians lived outside of Europe and North America, regions that a century ago included the majority of world Christians. An illustration of what has been happening in global church growth is revealed in statistics concerning church attendance. A Singapore theologian, Chee Pang Choong, tells me that church attendance research shows that there are now more people in church on Sunday morning in Indonesia than in all of the United Kingdom, Germany, and France combined.

The Anabaptist family of churches wherein I am a member is an example of the global transformations in church membership that most denominations are experiencing. As the twentieth century came to a close, there were more Anabaptists in Africa/Asia than in Europe/North America. Of the one million Anabaptists, only 45 percent were Euro-North Americans.[4]

Larry Miller, general secretary of Mennonite World Conference predicts, "Before the middle of the next century, churches in the south will play the primary role in shaping the direction of the Anabaptist-Mennonite movement." [5]

That is already happening. At the January 1997 meeting of the Mennonite World Conference in Calcutta, India, an Indonesian, Mesach Krisetya, was chosen as chairperson for the global assembly, and an Ethiopian, Bedru Hussein, was vice chairperson. This worldwide assembly comprises peoples from sixty countries and 192 conferences. A conference is an organized cluster of congregations.

These transformations are bringing surprising changes into all worldwide denominations. For example, in August 1998, Anglican bishops from around the world met in Lambeth in the United Kingdom for the global Anglican (Episcopal) bishops conference. The Lambeth Conference convenes every ten years. At this meeting Asian and African bishops had rather forthright counsel, especially regarding homosexuality. The subsequent statement did not condone homosexual practice. This was probably quite different than would have been the case had all the bishops been from an Anglo-Saxon culture.

The church is now the most authentic universal community on earth. I believe that the growth of the church around the world is the most significant historical development of the twentieth and twenty-first centuries. The reign of Jesus is indeed extending "from sea to sea and . . . to the ends of the earth" (Zech. 9:10; see ch. 8).

The second surprise: the church experiences suffering. As noted above, the church frequently suffers. Most of the first disciples of Jesus were martyred. The authorities sometimes opposed and occasionally persecuted and killed the Christians. This was true throughout the Roman Empire; it was also the case in other regions such as Persia or India. The Roman persecution occurred largely because Christians refused to worship or venerate the "genius" of the emperor. Christians insisted that there is only one Lord worthy of their ultimate loyalty and worship, and he is not the emperor; he is Jesus Christ.

The twentieth-century church also tasted suffering. Christians in the former Soviet Union and eastern Europe have occasionally told me their accounts of suffering: our pastor was sent to Siberia, they shot all the men and boys in our village who refused to sign a statement denying God, I lost my job, they tried to kill me by running a truck into my car, they knocked out all my teeth. Yet suffering does not extinguish the witness of the faithful church.

The third surprise: the church is touched with grace and joy. Wherever people celebrate the grace and forgiveness of Jesus, there is joy. Churches are not joyful because they are perfect communities; all churches have at least some cracks and unseemly difficulties. However, there is joy wherever people meet in Jesus' name and receive his gift of grace and forgiveness (Col. 3:15-17).

Singing is an expression of that joy. It is quite rare indeed for Christians to meet in worship and not sing. That is very different from gatherings such as one might see in a Muslim mosque or Buddhist temple. Muslims might chant eulogies at the time of Mohammed's birthday or in respect to one of their saints, but I have never heard Muslims sing at the times of formal worship when they are submitting themselves to God in prayer.

Yet it is almost unimaginable for Christians to gather for worship without expressing their joy in song. Muslims sometimes comment, "When Christians sing as they worship, it sounds as though they are having a party." That is true. Meeting in the name of Jesus is an invitation to a party filled with joy and song.

The fourth surprise: the church is surprisingly diverse. This is in dramatic contrast to a movement such as Islam; all Muslim formal prayer in all mosques in all language groups around the world is the same. That is not the case in the Christian gatherings; worship styles are exceedingly diverse, and Christians around the world worship in a couple thousand languages.

The diversity of the church is unsurprising. The church historian, Luke, specifically mentions fifteen languages and nations as present at the birthday of the church; he exults that people are there from "every nation under heaven" (Acts 2:5). Diversity became a defining characteristic of the church at its birthday when 3,000 people were baptized who represented nations far beyond Israel's boundaries. However, Luke notes that these believers were Jewish or converts to Judaism.

About fifteen years later an astonishing assembly developed in Antioch in Syria: Jewish and Gentile people were united in that church. So were believers from Europe, Asia, and Africa. In their traditional customs, Jews and Gentiles did not even eat together, unless the Gentiles took on the Jewish culture such as male circumcision and diet practices. Yet in Antioch the impossible was happening—a fellowship of many nationalities and traditions was forming.

The nonbelievers of Antioch were so astonished by this church, that they nicknamed this amazing assembly, Christians. The nickname stuck. To this day, followers of Jesus carry that nickname: Christians. The nonbelievers called the Antioch assembly "Christian," because it was a new creation; no other assembly in the city had such diversity and unity.

The modern diversity of the church was what I experienced when observing The World Council of Churches convocation in Nairobi, Kenya, in 1975. A bishop from the Syrian Orthodox Church spoke. He wore a long black robe, a large cross on his chest, and a black turban on his head. He told us that his church is 2,000 years old and every Sunday they worship in Aramaic, the same language Jesus spoke.

At that same World Council meeting a bishop was present from the African Israeli Church, Ninevah. He was dressed in colobus monkey skins, and his church choir sang in the Luo language with drums and exuberant dancing. That is diversity!

The World Council of Churches reveals the diversities between families of churches, such as the Syrian Orthodox or the

African Israeli Church Ninevah. However, even in church families, one experiences diversity.

Rich diversity permeated the 1997 Anabaptist/Brethren in the Christ/Mennonite assembly in Calcutta, already mentioned in this chapter. Probably 120 language groups were represented in that global assembly.

That assembly was a window into the rich diversity of the global church. For example, the Asian day worship included exquisite liturgical dancing. However, the American day featured gathering in small groups for a concert of prayer. The Europeans majored in metaphorical preaching and drama. During the African day an invitation was extended for people to be converted, and South Americans invited people to come forward for prayers of healing. The Calcutta assembly revealed a kaleidoscope of cultures and theologies that characterizes all world church assemblies today.

The fifth surprise: The church has unity. All Christian gatherings in all cultures and languages everywhere confess that Jesus Christ is Lord and Savior. That confession is universal among all Christian churches.

Yet the unity of the church is more profound than the glue a common confession provides. There is a special unity the Holy Spirit creates among those who meet together in Jesus' name. That unity is a bonding more enduring and precious than family ties. It is a unity that transcends denominational diversity.

I suppose that I have worshiped in Christian gatherings in about fifty countries, in dozens of different denominations. These gatherings have been as diverse as an all-night Zionist African traditional church in Swaziland to an incense-permeated Greek Orthodox Church in Greece with bells, vestments, and gorgeous liturgy. I have worshiped with Quakers where all was silent; I have also worshiped with Pentecostals where everyone prayed with great fervor all at the same time. Yet in all such diversities, I have always experienced the special bonding together that Jesus Christ creates.

This is why church divisions are so exceedingly painful. A political party might divide. That is quite expected. But for a church to divide is tearing apart the special unity that Jesus Christ creates. It is for this reason that the Scriptures command Christians, "Make every effort to keep the unity of the Spirit through the bond of peace" (Eph. 4:3).

Our world is divisive: nation against nation, labor against management, or culture against culture. However, societies expect the church to be different. There is an awareness, even outside the church, that the nature of the church nurtures diversity in the bonds of unity.

A few years ago a church community in Tanzania of about 30,000 members was experiencing a division. That break was along tribal lines. All African nations struggle to maintain harmony among their widely diverse languages and societies. In most nations the church is the most authentic inter tribal community. Therefore, if the church divides along tribal lines, the nation cannot survive. The health of the nation depends on the unity of the church.

It is, therefore, not surprising that the Muslim president of Tanzania met with leaders of this divided church. The president counseled, "Be the church. Preserve the unity of the church. Practice what your Bible teaches!"

The sixth surprise: the church has authority. In a dramatic act of trust and confidence Jesus once exclaimed to Peter and his disciples, "I will give you the keys of the kingdom of heaven" (Matt. 16:19). Jesus also said that those gathered in his name have the authority to bind and to loose (Matt. 16:19; 18:18).

What does it mean for the church to "bind and loosen"? One dimension is the authority to decide which cultural or social practices are right for the Christian and which are not. For example, nowhere does the Bible specifically demand that slave masters must free all of their slaves. The church universally had "bound" slavery; however, nowadays the church with authority insists that it is not permissible for a Christian to own slaves.

The authority Jesus gives the church "to bind and to loosen" is astonishing. The Chagga of Tanzania were grateful when they discovered that authority. A little over a century ago German Lutheran missionaries had translated portions of the Bible into the Chagga language, then headed back to Germany to write a book on how to be a missionary without changing a people's culture.

Alas, as the Chagga people studied the Gospel accounts of Jesus, they discovered that many of their practices were not good. The leaders called an assembly of believers, and made a covenant together to transform their practices. Alcohol devastated their homes, so they prohibited alcohol. Other things had to go as well: female circumcision, polygamy, witchcraft, and beating of one's wife. Homes had to be neat and clean, and so the Chagga leaders appointed inspectors to check up on household cleanliness.[6]

The Chagga church had exercised their authority to bind and loosen. The way the Chagga made their decisions was quite similar to a conference that the early church convened in Jerusalem. That noteworthy Jerusalem Conference (Acts 15) is an excellent example of the way the church should express its authority to bind and to loosen.

The diversity of the church in Antioch was described earlier in this chapter. Not everyone was keen about that diversity. Jewish believers in Jerusalem were very uneasy about Gentiles in the Antioch Church who did not practice Jewish customs. Consequently, church leaders met in Jerusalem to decide how to deal with cultural and religious differences between Gentiles and Jews.

The issue was whether Gentile Christians had to embrace Old Testament practices, like male circumcision. (At that time the Old Testament comprised the only Scriptures universally accepted by the church.)

With confidence, the assembly in Jerusalem exercised the authority Christ had given to the church. These were the steps they took as they searched for answers to the vexing issues of Gentile and Jewish religious and cultural practices.

- They convened a decision-making meeting with leaders representing both Jewish and Gentile churches.
- They shared accounts of the faith of Gentile believers.
- They interpreted Scriptures in the light of Jesus Christ.
- They prayerfully listened to the Holy Spirit's counsel.
- They made a decision they believed was in harmony with Jesus Christ and the Scriptures, the counsel of the Holy Spirit, their convictions, and preserving the unity of the church.

The Jerusalem assembly agreed that certain practices were not befitting for redeemed people. They cited the following as practices Christians should avoid: fornication, idol worship, eating meat offered as sacrifices to idols, and eating or drinking blood. As for other cultural practices, the assembly gave freedom. Even more important than their decisions is the way they made the decisions.

The Jerusalem Conference was a watershed. It freed Gentiles to become full members in the church without embracing Old Testament Jewish practices. It released the church to become a universal movement embracing all cultures, while also calling the church to its accountability to Christ and the Scriptures under the guidance of the Holy Spirit.

At the Jerusalem Conference the church had bound and loosened certain religious, cultural, and social practices. This was an exhilarating responsibility that the Jerusalem Conference, the Chagga Church, and multitudes of other Christian assemblies have exercised throughout the centuries.

The seventh surprise: members of the church converse with God. Prayer is conversation with God. Prayer is one of the mysteries of the Christian Way. God knows what we need; why, then, pray? Prayer is much more than bringing our requests to God. Prayer is also listening to God, communing with God, obeying God, learning to know God.

God delights in our prayers, and he moves as we pray. One can pray personally and alone; one can also join in prayer where two or three are gathered for worship and prayer; we can pray with and in the church gathered for worship; we can pray anywhere and at any time. In fact, a joy of the Christian Way is the privilege of living prayerfully all the time.

Prayer is conversation with God. This involves listening to God, and often involves sharing our concerns with God as well. Prayer is praising God for who he is, and thanking God for his blessings. Prayer involves confession of sin, and commitment to walking in obedience to God. God invites us to ask for guidance and wisdom (Col. 3:15-16; Philippians 4:4-7; James 1:5).

Bringing requests to God is one form of prayer. Jesus promised, "You may ask me for anything in my name, and I will do it" (John 14:14). Once Jesus exclaimed, "Again, I tell you that if two of you on earth agree about anything you ask for, it will be done for you by my Father in heaven" (Matt. 18:19).

These are remarkable promises. But God does not appreciate or answer greedy prayers. In fact, the Scriptures warn,

> You quarrel and fight. You do not have, because you do not ask God. When you ask, you do not receive, because you ask with wrong motives, that you may spend what you get on your pleasures. (James 4:2-3)

It is important to pray in harmony with God's will, for he knows what is best. Sometimes God's answer to our requests is a "no." When that happens, we need to accept that answer without resentment. God sees the big picture, and it is wise to accept his "yes" or "no." Of course, in prayer we might argue with God and even debate him. However, our deep desire should be to pray in harmony with God's will. We need to pray in faith that God does hear and answer prayer (James 1:6-8).

Jesus prayed in that way the night of his arrest, "My Father, if it is possible, may this cup be taken from me. Yet not as I will, but as you will" (Matt. 26:39).

As we discern God's will, we have the authority to pray with confidence. God revels in our prayers. The Scriptures use the metaphor of fragrant incense ascending to heaven to describe how God feels about our prayers; they smell good.

One depressing night in the O'Hare Airport in Chicago, I experienced God moving as I prayed. It was a foggy night in February, with some freezing rain. The airport was in bedlam because scores of departures were canceled. When I got to the gate for my Elkhart-bound flight, I discovered that it also had been canceled.

I walked some distance to the South Bend-bound gate, and discovered that they hoped to fly, although it was touch and go. I checked in, and sat down to think through a plan of action for getting from South Bend to Elkhart. It was late, about 10:30 p.m. My poor vision at night made it impossible for me to consider renting and driving a car through the fog and ice. I was ill, recovering from the flu and coughing.

I prayed, "Lord, what is the plan? I don't think you want me to sleep in an airport tonight because I am quite ill. I cannot drive. I hate to call anyone on a night like this to meet me at South Bend long after bedtime. What shall I do. Lord, please help me!"

Just then, a man with a red cap wended his way toward me through the crowd. "Hi, David Shenk," he exclaimed, "I am Ken Kauffman from Goshen."

My surprise was total as I asked, "When have we met?"

"Don't you remember?" Ken teased. "Thirty years ago, I was a freshman at Eastern Mennonite College and you were a senior."

How could Ken spot me in the bedlam of O'Hare? But he did and was flying to South Bend, where his daughter met him. They gladly drove out of their way along the treacherous back roads to take me to Elkhart on their way to Goshen.

"Ken," I said, "tonight God sent me an angel who was wearing a red cap."

Was this just a coincidence? What do you think?

Jesus invites us to pray. God welcomes our prayers. He delights in delighting us with his responses to our prayers.

The eighth surprise: Those who gather care for one another. Jesus said, "By this all men will know that you are my disciples, if you love one another" (John 13:35).

Loving care for one another was the distinguishing character of the church when it was first created. People shared their belongings so that no one was in need. Soon they appointed people with special responsibility to care for the widows. That first Jerusalem assembly was bonded together in love. The faithful church everywhere is a caring assembly.

Recently Grace and I were facing major decisions. We had a paralysis of will; we could not decide. Christian friends helped us see that our difficulty was related to some wounds that festered in us from the past and present circumstances. So we called four people from our assembly to meet with us, including the pastor. We confessed our sins of resentment. We named some of the wounds and the circumstances that contributed to those wounds. Tears flowed quite freely.

Then the four friends stood around us and prayed for forgiveness and healing. The pastor anointed us with oil, as they named each sin and wound. We experienced a deep healing and forgiveness. The burden became lighter. We were empowered to move on. We had experienced the church helping to bear our burdens.

Caring for one another should be earnest business for the Christian assembly. For example, as I am writing this paragraph, a family in my church is moving into another house. Many from our congregation are helping; Grace is taking prepared food for those involved in the moving party.

Our congregation has a "trouble fund." Whenever we assemble for worship, we invite people to give money as a joyful response to the gift of grace and forgiveness we receive from Jesus Christ. A percentage of those weekly offerings is placed in the trouble fund, so that the pastor and his team will always have funds to help people in need.

The caring ministry of the assembly reaches beyond the local church. For example, in January 1998 a terrible ice storm ravaged northern New York State, New England, and eastern Canada. For many days, there was no electricity. Churches acted quickly. In my church denomination there is an organization known as Mennonite Disaster Service (MDS). MDS contacted farmers outside of the disaster area and asked them to loan back-up generators for farms without electricity. They sent trucks from farm to farm to pick up generators, then trucked these machines to farms without electricity. In this way they helped to avoid catastrophe, especially on large dairy farms.

The Scriptures counsel, "Carry each others' burdens, and in this way you will fulfill the law of Christ" (Gal. 6:2).

The faithful church is a remarkable team; Christ is the captain and the Holy Spirit is the coach. This team is bonded in love; it is the family of God; it is the assembly of those who say yes to Jesus.

The final two chapters explore other dimensions of the Christian church. These include themes such as authority, mission, the interpretation of Scripture, discernment, invitation, and celebration. We will explore ways the church relates to society, cultures, and religions.

• • •

Jerusalem was "Exceedingly amazed!"

The Holy Spirit had come on the disciples of Jesus. The city and none of the thousands from other countries had ever seen or heard anything like it. They were "exceedingly amazed."

However, surprises do not always give us joy.

Imagine the devastating surprise of the crucifixion of Jesus Christ. The followers of Jesus had believed that he was the promised King and Messiah. They were utterly shattered in the astonishing disaster of his death.

However, their grief was transformed into great joy as new and astounding surprises touched them. Previous chapters have described the surprise of the resurrection of Jesus.

The other astonishment was the ascension of Jesus into heaven. Forty days later the Holy Spirit came on 120 disciples of Jesus who had gathered in a room in Jerusalem for a ten-day prayer meeting.

The inhabitants of the city ran to see and hear what was happening, and they were "exceedingly amazed!" The Holy Spirit surprised everyone, the disciples of Jesus and the throngs in Jerusalem. That was the day the church was created, a community formed through the mighty power of the Holy Spirit.

From those beginnings in Jerusalem, the church has grown to become the most authentic universal community on earth. Nevertheless, that growth is touched with suffering.

The coach and the team, the Holy Spirit and the church, these are the "exceedingly amazing" surprises that touched Jerusalem two millennia ago when the Holy Spirit came with power and the church was created. The work of the Holy Spirit and the creation of church, wherever that might be, is indeed a surprise of grace and power.

12

THE MESSAGE

Background Scripture: Matthew 28:16-20, Acts 1:6-8

Celsus rudely attacked the church and its message. He lived about 150 years after the birth of the church, described in the previous chapter. He was probably from Alexandria, in Egypt. He made sarcastic attacks against the church and its message.

For example, Celsus wrote that it is ridiculous and quite comical to think that God sent his Son to tiny insignificant Palestine into a Jewish family; if God wanted to impact the world he would have thought of much more significant places to send his Son.

However, Celsus despaired of stopping this silly Christian movement, because ordinary Christian people were in the habit of chatting about Jesus everywhere. They would not be stopped.

Celsus wrote,

We see in private houses, workers in wool and leather, washermen, and persons of the most uneducated and rustic kind . . . they get hold of the children privately and any women who are as ignorant as themselves. They then pour out wonderful statements . . . they whisper. . . . "If you like, you can come with the women and your play-mates to the women's quarters in the leather shop or the laundry, that you may get all there is." With words like these, they win them over.[1]

When even the Christian laundry women tell the household children about Jesus, how can one stop the growth of the church? For 2,000 years that has been the primary way the church has grown, people on the job living the way of Jesus and telling their colleagues about Jesus. The "see and tell" presence of the church as a people touched with grace and joy is also a winsome attraction.

However, quite frequently the church also sends missionaries into regions far away to tell people who have no Christian neighbors about Jesus Christ. Julian of Alexandria in Egypt was one such missionary. In the sixth century his home church in Alexandria commissioned Julian to tell the Noba people about Jesus Christ. He sailed up the Nile River far into Nubia (Sudan today).

Missionary Julian suffered from the heat. So for seven hours each day he rested in a water-filled cavern along the banks of the Nile. With only a linen cloth around his waist, he sat submerged in the water. Then when evening came, Julian would venture out of his cool water-filled cavern, dress appropriately, and preach to the Noba people.

As the Noba came to believe in Jesus, they formed assemblies. When Julian returned to Alexandria, quite a number of churches had been planted among the Noba people in Nubia.[2]

A Missionary Movement

The Christian practice of sharing the good news of Jesus Christ with people and inviting them to believe, repent, and be baptized began with the birth of the church described in the previous chapter. This is to say the church is a missionary movement; it is a community of joy with a message to share with all peoples everywhere. That is what Jesus expected the church should be, a people with a message for the whole world.

Before his ascension, Jesus startled his disciples by telling them,

All authority in heaven and on earth has been given to me. Therefore go and make disciples of all nations, baptizing them in the name of the Father and of the Son and of the Holy Spirit, and teaching them to obey everything I have commanded you. And surely I am with you always, to the very end of the age. (Matt. 28:18-20)

Christians refer to this command and promise as the "Great Commission!" Jesus also exclaimed, "As the Father has sent me, I am sending you. . . . Receive the Holy Spirit" (John 20:21, 22). Recall that Jesus' last words to his disciples before his ascension were, "But you will receive power when the Holy Spirit comes on you; and you will be my witnesses in Jerusalem, and in all Judea and Samaria, and to the ends of the earth" (Acts 1:8).

These commands, promises, and expectations to share the gospel with peoples around the world were no afterthought. Mission to the ends of the earth was at the center of Jesus' ministry from the moment the angel announced to his mother Mary that her son would establish David's kingdom forever. His whole life and ministry was consistent with that vision.

In fact, the universal mission of Jesus the Messiah and the church were the expectation and hope of biblical prophets for hundreds of years before the birth of Jesus. For example, the Prophet Isaiah, writing about 700 years before Christ, exclaimed, "In that day the Root of Jesse will stand as a banner for the peoples; the nations will rally to him, and his place of rest will be glorious" (Isa. 11:10). (Jesse was King David's father. Christians believe that the Root of Jesse refers to Jesus. Recall that Christians believe that Jesus is the King from David's line whom God promised would reign forever.)

Missionaries Might be Amusing!

Celsus scoffed at the ignorance of the laundry women who told the children of their employers about Jesus, and the Noba people were amused seeing Julian sitting in a water pool to escape Nubia's heat. Even today the church committed to proclaiming the message of Jesus Christ might be considered amusing or even ridiculous. Indeed missionaries do sometimes make humorous or even dreadful mistakes.

An embarrassing event for me occurred when I and my team hosted a banquet in a large restaurant in honor of Jewish guests. The Jewish religion prohibits eating pork. Alas, we had thoughtlessly ordered a pork entree. What a disaster! Happily the restaurant management quickly substituted chicken for our Jewish friends. We had a grand evening together.

The message is good news!

Even though the mistakes have been many, the church in mission proclaims good news. When my father and stepmother visited Bumangi where my parents had served as pioneer missionaries, the church killed a cow for the celebration feast.

At the celebration, Pastor Nyakitumu said, "Pastor and Mama Shenk made mistakes. Sometimes we laughed at their ways. However, they introduced us to Jesus Christ in whom we have salvation. The treasure of the gospel they brought us has blinded our eyes to the mistakes they made."

Jesus Christ in his fullness is the message that the faithful church proclaims. The Holy Spirit calls the church to express that message through the qualities of its life together as an assembly who meet in Jesus' name. The church also expresses the message through its ministries of compassion and through its witness that Jesus Christ is Lord and Savior.

The Scriptures

As the early church moved from society to society in mission, the Christians quickly recognized the need for Scriptures. All they had at first were the Jewish Scriptures that Christians later referred to as the Old Testament. (The Old Testament was first written in Hebrew; by the time of Jesus there was also a Greek translation known as the Septuagint.)

Writings about Jesus and the church

However, the church in mission also needed reliable accounts of the life and teaching of Jesus and instructions for the newly forming churches. This was especially urgent because legends would quickly distort the real life of Jesus. People imagined a lot; for example, some said that as a child Jesus made clay birds, blew on them, and they became alive. Plenty of those kinds of tales began to circulate early on. The church needed trustworthy Scriptures to proclaim the message of Jesus Christ with confidence.

One of the most significant priorities was acquiring reliable accounts of the life of Jesus Christ. Scholars believe that very early a brief but trustworthy written account of the life and teachings of Jesus was circulating among the churches. Scholars have called this document *Quelle,* meaning source. However, the church needed more than *Quelle,* and so in time four accounts were written and accepted as Scripture.

These are included in the Christian Bible. These accounts of the life, ministry, and teaching of Jesus are called the Gospels (Matthew, Mark, Luke, and John). *Gospel* means good news.

Scholars debate the completion date of each of the four Gospels. There is credible scholarly opinion that all four Gospels were written within four decades of the church's Pentecost beginning. That would be not later than A.D. 70. But other credible scholars argue for up to six decades after Pentecost with Mark the first (c. A.D. 50) and John the last (c. A.D. 90). Most scholars had assumed that Mark was written first; in recent years that assumption has been challenged by some scholars who argue that John or Matthew was written before Mark.[3]

Other New Testament Scriptures include Acts, a history of the early church. In addition, there are twenty-three letters written to Christian assemblies or church leaders. All of these New Testament documents were written in Greek, the language of international communication throughout the Middle East region at the time of Jesus.

A debate: which writings?

It took some time for the church as a whole to reach agreement about which books should be included in their Scriptures. Modern biblical scholars have found a list (canon) of books dated about A.D. 200. Five books were not in that list that were later included in the New Testament: Hebrews, James, 1 and 2 Peter, and 3 John. However, by about A.D. 300, the church as a whole had come to an agreement concerning its Scriptures.

It might be surprising that a controversy developed in the church during the second century about the Old Testament. Marcion, a Christian leader from Asia Minor, insisted that the God of the Old Testament is a different God than the God of the New Testament. He was also opposed to Jewish influence in the church. For these reasons he taught that the Old Testament should be rejected by Christians.

The conflict on this matter became very intense. However, the church as a whole rejected Marcion's teachings. The Old Testament remained a part of the Christian Scriptures.

The Christian Bible was formed

By about A.D. 300, the church had come to accept both the Old Testament and the New Testament as Scriptures. The confidence of the church in the leadership of apostles helped the selection process. Apostle refers to a person to whom the Holy Spirit and the church have given authority to lead and teach the church. The first apostles were leaders in the church who had been disciples of Jesus during his ministry.

The books the church accepted as Scripture were written by apostles who had been with Jesus or persons close to the ministry of the first apostles. For example, although Mark was not one of the first apostles, his gospel was accepted because of the belief that Mark received information and counsel from the apostle Peter, who had been one of the twelve disciples of Jesus.

The decision about the list of books to be included in the New Testament happened without strife; the books included were already widely circulated and read throughout the church and considered to be Scripture. (Note, however, that the Ethiopian canon has some differences. We have also noted the controversy about the Old Testament.)

The church believes that those who wrote these Scriptures, the Old and New Testament, were inspired by the Spirit of God. The missionary Paul wrote to a young pastor, Timothy, saying, "All Scripture is God-breathed and is useful for teaching, rebuking, correcting and training in righteousness" (2 Tim. 3:16).

However, this is a question people often ask: are the accounts trustworthy? That is an important question. If the Christian faith were primarily moral values or a philosophy, the question of trustworthy accounts would be irrelevant. For example, if Hindus were to discover that the Krishna narratives never happened, that would not in the least affect the value of the narratives; their value is the philosophy they convey. However, the Christian faith is built on the real acts of God in real history and it invites commitment to a real person, Jesus of Nazareth, whom the church confesses to be the Christ.

Myth or Truth

If the accounts of Jesus are another Santa Claus myth, it is ridiculous to commit one's life to him. A person will give himself to a person or cause he believes is true. A person should not base his life on a fairy tale.

Today there is a widespread assumption in Euro/North American culture that the gospel accounts are mythical and legendary, a kind of fairy tale. The Jesus Seminar in North America proclaims the notion that there is really no way to get in touch with the real Jesus. These scholars meet occasionally and their opinions are often proclaimed by the press; trustworthy gospel accounts is not their cup of tea. Wherever such notions prevail that consider the Jesus of the biblical Scriptures to be a myth or legend, the message of the church withers. One cannot invite people to commit their lives to a fairy tale.

Is Jesus a myth or has God indeed sent his real Son into the real world? This question is so fundamental that we shall look at the evidence quite carefully. Are the New Testament accounts trustworthy? Jesus himself pled with those who did not believe in him to look at the evidence (John 5:31-40; 10:38). Following are several statements of evidence that relate to the question: are the accounts trustworthy?

1. *The accounts include embarrassing episodes.* Here are several examples of embarrassing failures that are included in the accounts.

Peter denied Jesus three times the night of his arrest and trial.

The disciples argued with one another concerning who was the greatest at the Passover meal just before Jesus was arrested.

Women were the first to meet Jesus after his resurrection; the men were hiding and fearful. The cultural expectation would be that the women would be hiding and the brave men would be the first to go and check out the tomb. Furthermore, in Jewish society, the witness of men concerning an event was much more respected than the witness of women. If there was any inclination to alter the accounts to appear favorable or to "prove" a point, the authors would not have included such embarrassing details.

2. *The accounts include outrageous claims by Jesus.* The writers would never have included such outrageous claims if they were interested in being credible with either Gentiles or Jews.[4] Even the disciples themselves were scandalized with the claims Jesus made; it took staunchly monotheistic Peter a couple of years of association with Jesus before he would dare say to Jesus: you are the Son of the Living God.

Consider some of the claims Jesus either made or accepted as true: he was the Son of God, the Lamb of God, the light of the world, the Word who is God, the way, the truth, the life, the Son of man, Lord and God, Immanuel, the resurrection, the Good Shepherd, the one with all authority in heaven and earth, before Abraham was I am, one with the Father, no one comes to the Father but by me, follow me! Such shocking statements were not the way to get a hearing with either Jewish or Gentile people.

3. *The accounts describe Jesus as surprisingly human.* M. Scott Peck points out that this reveals that the authors of the Gospels did not embellish Jesus.[5] Jesus expressed a touch of impatience with his mother. He was often frustrated and deeply impatient. He cried. He got angry. In deep anger he strode into the temple and overturned the tables of the merchants and scattered the money across the floor. He got thirsty, hungry, and tired. He enjoyed feasting.

Jesus called his self-righteous opponents nasty things like a brood of vipers, children of the devil, whitewashed sepulchers, or blind guides. He scandalized the religious leaders by letting a sinful woman kiss his feet, wash them with her tears, and dry them with her hair.

These are not the sort of things editors put into print if they are attempting to create a pious saint. Legends also wash such human feelings and offensive statements out of the account. Not so with the Gospel writers. The Jesus they describe is no meek and mild angel with a halo. He is a man with gutsy feelings, yet sinless. He is a real man and a righteous man.

4. *Political, religious, geographical, historical, and cultural data are accurate.* Archaeology and nonbiblical manuscripts demonstrate that the accounts of political and Jewish religious history are accurate. The same is true of descriptions of culture and geography. For example, many scholars have assumed that John developed his gospel to fit into a Greek world view. However, in recent years the Dead Sea Scrolls have showed that John's world view was thoroughly Jewish. John's Gospel speaks with astonishing relevancy into a significant stream of Jewish culture and thinking at the time of Jesus.[6]

Luke's historical data is remarkable. Tradition identifies him as a medical doctor, and he had a knack for research and history. He wrote both the Gospel of Luke and the early church history known as Acts. Here is an impressive example of his accuracy.

In the fifteenth year of the reign of Tiberius Caesar—when Pontius Pilate was governor of Judea, Herod was tetrarch of Galilee, his brother Philip was tetrarch of Iturea and Traconitis, and Lysanias was tetrarch of Abilene—during the high priesthood of Annas and Caiaphas... (Luke 3:1-2).

These were complex political situations. Luke was so careful with the political history, surely he exercised at least equal care in researching and accurately recording events related to Jesus and the early Christian movement.

5. *The manuscripts include some problems.* On the other hand, in the previous chapter we described the ascension of Jesus. Matthew states that Jesus met his disciples at a mountain in Galilee where he gave them the great commission. Luke states that the ascension happened near Bethany in Judea, about 75 miles south of Galilee. That is a riddle. Probably the disciples returned the 75 miles to Jerusalem and Bethany after meeting Jesus at the mountain in Galilee. However, the texts leave us wondering; we are not sure how to put it all together.

In a court of law, these kinds of riddles in the testimony of witnesses are evidence that the witnesses have not fabricated the story. When the incident is invented, the witnesses get together and plan to say exactly the same thing, and clarify all potential problems. However, minor riddles in the accounts of witnesses, enhance the confidence that the witnesses are giving an authentic and trustworthy account of the incident as they perceived it.

That same principle holds true in the Gospel accounts. The challenge of reconciling all details of the four Gospel accounts strengthens confidence in the trustworthiness of the writers and what they have recorded. There was no collusion.

6. *The letters to the churches and church leaders, as well as the book of Acts, also contain significant information about Jesus.* These letters also help provide a portrait of Jesus; that

portrait is consistent with the Gospel accounts. For example, Peter mentions God declaring that Jesus is his beloved Son when several of the disciples were with Jesus on a mountain (2 Pet. 1:16-18). Matthew, Mark, and Luke each describe that event. Peter's letter provides additional insight into the significance of that event.

7. *The large number of manuscripts is significant.* There are at least fragments of some 5,000 ancient New Testament manuscripts. Scholars assure us that our modern New Testament Scriptures are accurate transmissions of the earliest manuscripts. A biblical scholar, F. J. A. Hort, states that the possibility that a word or phrase is different than the original text is only 1 in 1,000. [7]

8. *Finally, study of early texts strengthens confidence in the reliability of the accounts.* In recent years a team of Jewish biblical scholars at the Hebrew University in Jerusalem, under the leadership of David Flusser, has invested special attention in the Gospel of Mark. The Greek used in Mark is not smooth flowing. This has perplexed scholars. As an experiment, the Flusser team has translated every Greek word directly into Aramaic. (That is the language Jesus and his disciples spoke.) The consequence is smooth idiomatic Aramaic.[8]

The Flusser team is persuaded that the original book of Mark was in Aramaic, and that they have an accurate transcription of that original Aramaic. Apparently those who translated the original book of Mark into Greek translated every Aramaic word literally. That is why the Greek version is so rough; they probably did not want to corrupt the original Scripture.

Flusser and his team believe that the Aramaic Gospel of Mark is an account of Jesus that brings us right next to Jesus and his disciples. In the jargon of historical research, we call this a primary document. Historians take primary documents very seriously when they want to ascertain the trustworthiness of a narrative.

Strands of Evidence

Jesus and New Testament writers invite us to examine the evidence as we consider this question: who is Jesus Christ? As a response to this biblical invitation to explore the evidence, I have described eight strands of evidence that lend confidence in the reliability of the New Testament accounts concerning Jesus Christ.

The concept of evidence is familiar to us in our modern cultures that are significantly influenced by the search for reliable data that scientific methodology demands. Modern science searches for data and builds scientific theories on the evidence that the data provides. The Christian Way is also founded on data and the evidence that the data provides.

Jesus himself strongly encouraged people to examine the data and evidence and respond in faith to the truth that the evidence supports (John 6:31-47). Several New Testament writers specifically acknowledge the fundamental significance of evidence and accuracy in their communication of the gospel.

For example Luke writes,

> Many have undertaken to draw up an account of the things that have been fulfilled among us, just as they were handed down to us by those who from the first were eyewitnesses and servants of the word. Therefore, since I myself have carefully investigated everything from the beginning, it seemed good also to me to write an orderly account for you, most excellent Theophilus, so that you may know the certainty of the things you have been taught. (Luke 1:1-4)

John explains why he has written:

> Jesus did many other miraculous signs in the presence of his disciples, which are not recorded in this book. But these are written that you may believe that Jesus is the Christ, the Son of God, and that by believing you may have life in his name. . . . (John 20:30-31)

This is the disciple who testifies to these things and who wrote them down. We know that his testimony is true. (John 21:24)

The Holy Spirit Inspired

Such evidence is not the whole story. Christians believe that the Holy Spirit inspired the writers of the biblical Scriptures. That is a confession of faith. It is a statement of belief.

Luke was a careful historian to be sure, but Christians believe that he did not write alone. The Holy Spirit was also involved, "breathing" on Luke as he penned the words and paragraphs that comprise Luke and Acts. This quality of divine inspiration leads the church to confess that the Bible is the Word of God written in human idiom and culture.

Personal Responses

Of course, having said all of this about the trustworthiness of the Gospel accounts, Jesus calls for personal decision. Everywhere that the gospel is proclaimed people are faced with a decision. Either they reject or believe in Jesus. His presence is and was a confrontation that requires a decision.

We see Jesus through the lens of our response to him. During his ministry some asserted that Jesus was of the Devil, and others believed that he was the promised Messiah. That same kind of divide is present in every society where Jesus is introduced. He is the great divide of human history.

One cannot be neutral about Jesus.

"Objection," a friend once exclaimed. "I am neutral about Jesus. I don't reject Jesus; I just ignore him; he has no relevance to my life!"

Is that really neutral? When I am in the presence of a person and try to get his attention but he ignores me, I experience that as rejection, not neutrality. Anyone who has heard the story of Jesus cannot be neutral about Jesus. Ignoring Jesus is rejection.

Those who believe that Jesus is Lord view his life and ministry very differently than do those who do not believe. For example, Thomas Jefferson, the author of the American Declaration of Independence, was a deist. He believed God created the earth, but that God is not involved any more in either human history or nature. We are on our own.

With such notions, Jefferson experienced Jesus to be incomprehensible, so he cut out all the miracles of Jesus that are recorded in the Gospels and then pasted scraps of some of Jesus' teachings together. He called his cut-and-pasted-together New Testament, *Philosophy of Jesus*. In Jefferson's Gospel, Jesus was crucified, but he did not rise from the dead.

Nonbelievers, both in the New Testament and in modern times, pass the word around that the disciples must have stolen the body of Jesus from the tomb and then made up the accounts about his resurrection. On the other hand, believers see in the resurrection astonishing joy and hope; they believe that they will also rise from the dead some day. All agree that there is an empty tomb, but they have totally opposite interpretations of the meaning of that event.

For this reason, the Gospels are much more than just historical data. The events are recorded, but the faith or rejection response to the events are also interwoven in the describing of the event.

Translations

As soon as the list of New Testament Scriptures was completed, Christians began translating the whole Bible, Old and New Testaments, into languages of the peoples among whom they lived. Probably the first translation was into Syriac in Syria. Soon Egyptians had translated the Bible into three Egyptian dialects, the Ethiopians into Geez, and the Romans into Latin.

As Christians carried the gospel into remote regions, translation of the Scriptures became a priority. When missionaries from Edessa in Mesopotamia traveled 6,000 miles to China in the sixth century, they translated the New Testament into the Chinese language. In the fourth century, Ufilas, who was living among the Goths in central Europe, reduced the Gothic language to writing and then translated the Bible into their language. In the sixth century, Christians translated the New Testament into the Chinese language.

Ufilas was the pioneer of agencies such as Wycliffe and its sister organization, the Summer Institute of Linguistics. Just as Ufilas did, these modern mission agencies focus on developing writing for unwritten languages, then translating the Bible into these languages.

Today ninety-eight percent of the people on earth have at least some of the Bible in their first language. The whole or part of the Bible is available in over 2,000 languages. Mission and Bible translation go hand in hand.

To translate the biblical Scriptures into the language of a people is to empower those people for astounding change.

A Revolutionary Book

The Bible is especially revolutionary because that book introduces people to Jesus.

An acquaintance was driving into Romania during the communist regime.

The border guard asked, "Do you have any Bibles?"

"Yes, I have my personal Bible," the traveler responded.

The guard went berserk shouting, "Dangerous thing in this car!" Guards ran towards the car with guns at the ready.

The guard was right. The Bible is dangerous. In the course of time it was the prayer assemblies of disciples of Jesus who peacefully confronted the Romanian regime. That confrontation contributed significantly to the collapse of the communist government in Romania.

Whenever the Bible is placed in the language of a people, those people are enabled to invite Jesus Christ into their own culture and idiom. Jesus empowers those who believe in him to transform their culture and society for good. These believers become "salt" and "light" in their society (Matt. 5:13-16).

Jesus Christ is the Center

Wherever people study the Bible they discover in fresh ways that Jesus is Lord. Neither church institutions nor political and economic powers have ultimate authority. Only Jesus is Lord. Christians confess that Jesus Christ is the central figure of human history and the biblical Scriptures.

Jesus himself made this point, exclaiming to the religious authorities,

> You diligently study the Scriptures because you think that by them you possess eternal life. These are the Scriptures that testify about me, yet you refuse to come to me to have life. (John 5:39,40)

Whenever we embrace the Scriptures or church traditions in a way that sidelines Jesus Christ, who is the central figure of the Scriptures, we sideline as well the center. Jesus is the center; therefore it is wise to interpret the Bible in the light of Jesus Christ.

A Christ-centered approach to the study of the Bible is called a Christocentric hermeneutic. We interpret all the Scriptures, both Old Testament and New Testament, in a Christ-centered way. That approach to the Scriptures is life-giving and helps yield accurate interpretation..

Jesus Christ is the ultimate surprise of all history, and he is most certainly the central surprise of the Bible!

• • •

Karl Barth is one of the most influential German theologians of the twentieth century. He had a keen commitment to the mission of the church.

It is said that news reporters in the United States asked him to share his most profound theological thought.

"Jesus loves me, this I know, for the Bible tells me so!" exclaimed Barth. People were astounded that Barth chose to quote from a simple song that children learn in Sunday school. Barth was right. That is the astonishing center and message of the Bible–Jesus loves me.

God's amazing plan is that every person on earth hear this good news. God's Spirit seeks to invite every person to receive this good news. God needs the church to help his grand plan succeed. That is the mission of the church.

13

THE BANQUET

Background Scripture: Luke 15:11-32

Jesus enjoyed banquets. In fact, he compared the kingdom he was establishing to a wedding party or a host inviting all his neighbors to enjoy a great feast.

One of Jesus' banquet stories was about a father and his two sons who operated the family farm estate together (Luke 15:11-31).

The way I relate to this story is influenced by the many years I have lived in cultures that were similar to the one where this story happened. Kenneth E. Bailey and Henri J. M. Nouwen have also influenced my comments.[1] Bailey has lived in the Middle East; Nouwen was a Dutch Catholic theologian and writer.

A Father and His Sons

The younger son gave his father tremendous grief when he demanded, "Father, give me my share of the estate."

Estates are divided at the time of the death of a parent. When the estate is mostly farmland and property, every effort is made to keep the operation intact. Often sons will farm the estate jointly after the father is deceased.

The younger son's request was ruthless, cruel, and evil. It was an unstated but obvious wish that his father would die. Furthermore, the son's demand required cash; he could not carry away half the farm. Imagine the financial turmoil the demand brought into the family business, especially with the exorbitant usury money lenders charged.

Nevertheless, the father gave the son his share of the estate. Although he grieved deeply, he respected his son's freedom to bring near ruinous damage on the family enterprise. Bailey observes that the suffering reached beyond the estate. Families in the nearby villages depended on estate-related enterprises for their livelihood. The economic crisis in the estate surely hurt the village people who depended on the estate for their livelihood. Nevertheless, the father accepted his son's rejection, knowing full well that his younger son wished him dead.

The son left. The wealth he carried with him was the accumulation of many generations of family enterprise. He took that family wealth and squandered it with wild living. When the money was depleted, he got a job feeding pigs, and wished the owner would allow him to eat the pig food, for he was hungry. He had hit "skid row."

Back home, the father yearned for his son. It is likely that he sent servants from time to time to visit his son and tell him that his father was ready to receive him back home whenever he decided to return. We imagine that day by day the father stood on a knoll looking into the far distance hoping to see his son walking home.

Finally the son decided on a scheme. He would return home and work for his father as a hired servant. In a ridiculous escape into fantasy, the son rationalized that in that way he could make amends for what he had done. By becoming a servant to his father, he could compensate for the great loss he had caused. So the son began his journey home, rehearsing over and over the speech he would make when he met his father.

In Middle Eastern countries there is usually a little village on the roadway at the border of estates. One day the father saw his son coming toward him far beyond the village homes clustered at the roadway boundary of the estate. The father ran down the road right through the village to welcome his son.

Middle Eastern men wore skirts in those days. To run, the father had to pull the skirt upward and tuck it into his belt, exposing his bare legs. The father ran through the village with his legs exposed, which was a most undignified spectacle for a man of his standing to behave.

The father embraced his son. He would not even hear his confessions and contrition. The son's scheme of repayment was ridiculous, in any event, for a lifetime of slavery would never compensate for the harm the son had caused to the family, the community, and the estate.

Rembrandt's original painting, *The Return of the Prodigal Son*, hangs in the Hermitage in Saint Petersburg, Russia. On a cold fall day in 1998, Grace and I sat in front of that painting encountering the message Rembrandt communicates in that provocative portrayal of the embrace of the father for his lost son. Twelve years earlier Henri J. M. Nouwen had invested many hours in the Hermitage reflecting on the painting; he has written about that encounter. His insights contributed to my own encounter with that Rembrandt painting.

Nouwen observed that the father's right hand is soft and seems to be the hand of a mother. The left hand is rough and broad, masculine looking. The father in the account expresses both mother and father love.[2] The loving parent is the center of the drama.

The son was clad in dirty, smelly, tattered clothes. He was barefoot. His feet were dusty and bruised from many miles of walking. The father, who just a few minutes earlier had abandoned his dignity as he ran through the village to meet his son, would not let his son walk through the village with the indignity of tattered clothing and bare feet; slaves walked barefooted.

The father and son wept together on the road just beyond the village. Villagers stood around them making snide comments about the irresponsible and cruel son. The father urged his servants to run with haste to bring the best robe in the house for the son to wear. They also brought him a pair of sandals.

Right on the spot, the father also placed a ring on his son's hand, a sign of authority, ownership, and sonship.

Surely the villagers had suffered the ripple effects from the acute financial turmoil of the estate in the wake of the son's departure. However, the father protected the son from the scorn of the villagers as he walked with his well-dressed son wearing the finger ring of family authority and the best robe in the father's household, the one that the father himself wore only on the most special occasions. The son's bruised and cracked feet were protected by new sandals. Father and son walked through the village in dignity.

Quickly the servants slaughtered a fattened calf. The father threw a great feast to welcome his son home. The whole community was invited, including the incredulous villagers.

Nevertheless, a deep sadness drifted through the feast, for the older son was not present. The custom was that the oldest son always sat beside his father at household feasts. Father and the oldest son always hosted feasts together; it had to be that way. However, the older son was not present; his place was conspicuously empty. Amid the joy and celebration everyone knew that the seat of the co-host was vacant.

Certainly the father had gone out to the fields to tell his older son the good news of his brother's return, and to invite him to take his place by his father for the welcome home feast. The older son ignored the invitation, choosing rather to embarrass his father. In fact, he planned to make a scene just at the time when the feast was in full swing. He delayed coming to the house until the feast was well underway.

When he came in from the fields midway through the feast, he called a servant to ask what was going on, although he already knew. He used the occasion to rant against his father. The father left his seat to plead with his older son to join the feast. The father was already embarrassed by the absence of this son from the seat at his side. Although the feast was underway, the older son berated and publicly shamed his father.

In anger the older son exclaimed,

Look! All these years I've been slaving for you and never disobeyed your orders. Yet you never gave me even a young goat so I could celebrate with my friends. But when this son of yours who has squandered your property with prostitutes comes home, you kill the fattened calf for him. (Luke 15:29-30)

The grieved father responded,

My son, you are always with me, and everything I have is yours. But we had to celebrate and be glad, because this brother of yours was dead and is alive again; he was lost and is found. (Luke 15:31)

Jesus told this story at a time when the religious authorities were becoming most distressed about the company Jesus was keeping. "Sinners" were surrounding Jesus, and following him everywhere.

Those who heard the story pondered its meaning. Who is the father? Who is the younger son? Who is the older son?

The father is God as revealed in Jesus Christ.

We are the sons who embarrass, avoid, or reject God. Some of us have squandered our lives in rebellion against God. Others are religious and think we are close to God. Yet we never participate in the banquet of joy God intends for us to enjoy, and we reject "sinners." We consider some people unworthy of God and our religious community. Nevertheless, God graciously invites us all to join him at the banquet.

Both sons thought they should earn the right to enjoy a feast with their father. However, we cannot earn the right to be at the banquet; the younger son could never repay his father for squandering the family estate. The older son worked like a slave yet never felt he had done well enough to deserve a banquet. But the father provided the banquet, because he loved his sons.

The father provided a clean and elegant robe for the son who entered the banquet. In fact, he provided the robe even before the banquet, when they were still far from their home. The father's elegant robe covered the tattered and soiled clothing of his son as they walked through the village toward their home. At the banquet the son is dressed with fine and dignified clothing.

The father offered a joyous feast to both sons, the "righteous" elder son and the "rebellious" younger son as well. The older son was invited to host the feast with his father; he refused. In the story it was the irresponsible son who was at the banquet; the responsible son was ranting outside.

The Banquet and Religions

For many years I have worked with a global missions program. Our missionaries served among atheists, Buddhists, Hindus, Muslims, Jews, Confucianists, secularists, animists, and people of other religions and ideologies as well. People often ask why we send missionaries to serve among very religious people, like Muslims. If people are religious, why would we encourage them to accept the Christian faith?

Throughout the chapters of this exploration of surprises of the Christian Way, we discerned significant differences between the Christian Way and other ways. One example is the Christian hope of the bodily resurrection of the dead. That is quite distinctively Christian. In fact, faiths such as Buddhism and Hinduism invite a totally opposite goal for human destiny: personal oblivion.

Nevertheless, the most surprising gift the Christian faith offers in a world of many religions and ideologies is the exceedingly amazing announcement that God is like the father in the story of the two sons and their father. It is only in Jesus Christ that we discover God to be like the father in that story. That is the core reason, the compelling reason, the compassionate reason that the church is involved in mission in other religions. God is that Father.

Other religions and philosophies never imagine that God would love us like that father loved his sons. For example, in

Hinduism the avatars (incarnations of God) come to earth to help the righteous, not the sinners.

In Islam, God is merciful to the righteous, but rejects sinners. A person who sins must do extra prayers to receive the mercy of God.

Buddha taught that there is no god to help us; we must acquire our own salvation.

In African Traditional Religion, God has gone away and will never return.

In Marxism, the dictatorship of the working classes is the ultimate authority that establishes utopia on earth; our twentieth century has discovered that the Marxist utopia is most often a taste of hell, not utopia.

In Jesus Christ, though, we discover that God is like the father in that story. That is the good news of the gospel that the church is called to proclaim and express among peoples everywhere, regardless of what their religion or philosophy might teach.

In Jesus Christ we discover "God is love" (1 John 4:16).

People everywhere should know that is the truth. Jesus declared that God's plan is that all peoples everywhere have the opportunity of knowing how much he loves them. In fact, the destiny of human history is linked to the worldwide proclamation of the gospel.

Jesus astounded his disciples by exclaiming, "And this gospel of the kingdom will be preached in the whole world as a testimony to all nations, then the end will come" (Matt. 24:14).

God seeks to invite every person throughout the whole world to his banquet. In the last chapter of the Bible we read, "Come! Whoever is thirsty, let him come; and whoever wishes, let him take the free gift of the water of life" (Rev. 22:17).

The Banquet and Cultures

Most often people will not object to a Christian mission that shares God's love, but they are deeply disturbed by a mission that upsets and changes cultures. The church in mission pleads "guilty" to that charge. Jesus Christ disturbed Jewish society profoundly. Recall his collision with the temple authorities when he chased the merchants, cows, sheep, and pigeons into the streets in a confusing melee. Likewise, wherever Jesus is proclaimed and received, he upsets things. A society is never the same after a people have said yes to Jesus Christ.

Of course, we are distressed that sometimes the changes the church in mission introduces into a culture have nothing to do with Jesus Christ, but rather are an expression of the cultural arrogance of the missionary. That is tragic and wrong, robbing a people of their culture in order that they might become Americanized or Koreanized or Anglicized Christians, or whatever the culture of the missionaries might be. James Michener's famous book, *Hawaii*, (1960) has popularized the wrongs of missionary imperialism.

However, in my judgment, that critique is often quite overstated. Arrogant and culturally insensitive missionaries are most often rejected by the people among whom they serve; their influence on the local culture is less than one might expect.

A principle of cultural change is that people accept only the changes they want to accept. For example, Lithuania was under Soviet communist rule for half a century. People submitted to communism, but most never accepted it. Less than a decade after the collapse of this system, it is hard to find a Lithuanian communist anywhere.

Jesus is who creates authentic revolution. This revolution is based on voluntary choice, never on force. It is a powerful and far-reaching revolution. It is a revolution based on love.

If God loves as Jesus loved, then any people who embrace Jesus are also embracing life-giving changes. In fact, the assembly that meets in Jesus' name is, by its very nature, a community of change and transformation. That was true from the very first day that the church was created nearly 2,000 years ago, and is equally true today.

To illustrate is an event that I observed as a child living with my parents at Bumangi among the Zanaki people of Tanzania.

Wakuru

Illiterate Wakuru was about twelve when she first came to visit our home.

She said, "I want to study the Bible."

My parents arranged for her to participate in a young women's Bible study group. Some weeks later she confided, "My father has arranged for me to marry an old polygamous man. The cows for the dowry have already been paid. What shall I do?" My parents would not tell her what to do. However, they did assure her that Jesus loves her; he offers her the gift of abundant life.

Armed only with that weapon of truth, Wakuru told her parents that she had decided not to marry that man, for she had discovered that Jesus loved her. Jesus would not choose for her to marry that man.

The battle was joined. The Zanaki tribal culture quaked. Never before had a young girl felt empowered to dissent from a marriage arranged by her father, and especially when the prospective husband had already paid the dowry. Wakuru was chained as a prisoner in her home and beaten. Lives were threatened. The battle raged for many months.

When alone in her mother's home where she was imprisoned, shackled with heavy brass bracelets to keep her from going anywhere, Wakuru sang quietly.

> There's not a friend like the lowly Jesus
> > No not one! No not one!
> None else could heal all our soul's diseases
> > No not one! No not one!
> Jesus knows all about our struggles,
> > he will guide till the day is done,
> There's not a friend like the lowly Jesus,
> > No not one! No not one!

In the dark prison of her mother's windowless grass thatched, mud and wattle hut, Wakuru was filled with joy and hope as she sang. She was having a banquet with Jesus Christ, her savior. Unknown to her the tiny new Christian assembly at Bumangi prayed fervently. Finally the parents relented; Wakuru was freed from that engagement.

Then when she was about 18, a Christian man, Nyakitumu, asked Wakuru for marriage. She was delighted, but her parents adamantly opposed the proposal. Nyakitumu was of the blacksmith clan and Wakuru was of the basket maker clan. The Zanaki tribe was divided between these two clans and it was taboo to intermarry.

The couple informed the parents that in Jesus Christ there was neither Jew nor Greek, to use a New Testament term. This meant there were no clan divisions that would prevent their marriage. Christ in his reconciling love removed such obstacles.

The parents would not relent in their opposition. The church met with the couple in prayer, and waited for the Spirit of God to change the parent's opposition. After many months, the parents did consent to the marriage. However, the elders of the Zanaki tribe cursed the couple so that they would never have children.

As I recall, Nyakitumu and Wakuru had the first Christian wedding in the newly developing Christian assembly among the Zanaki people. They were blessed with 13 children.

In 1998 I received a letter from Nyakitumu and Wakuru telling of their fiftieth wedding anniversary. The couple's children bought them new clothing. They walked in procession for a mile. The church was packed. Choirs sang. One choir was made up of their family, now including thirty-one grandchildren. Friends and pastors traveled great distances to join the celebration. The church rocked with joy. They killed a cow for the feast with six hundred guests joining in the celebration.

I am certain that this is the first fiftieth wedding anniversary ever celebrated among the Zanaki people. In polygamous societies, such an event never happened. It is no wonder that the whole community was baptized with joy as they witnessed this anniversary event.

That couple and others like them transformed the Zanaki culture and society in surprising ways. Yet it was not they alone who brought about the transformation; it was Jesus Christ through the Holy Spirit who empowered them, and the church who encouraged them.

The Banquet Is at Hand

The kingdom of God is a banquet. The banquet has begun. Wherever people gather in Jesus' name celebrating his grace and forgiveness, there is joy. Churches everywhere that celebrate the grace of Jesus Christ are communities of joy.

Churches are also communities of the future, for Jesus has promised to come back again at history's climax. He has promised to fulfill the kingdom he inaugurated 2,000 years ago. His kingdom has begun; the church around the world is a sign that the kingdom of Jesus Christ is extending to the ends of the earth. These communities of the kingdom scattered around the world are assemblies of hope, for they believe Jesus is coming again to consummate and fulfill the kingdom of God forever.

The appetizer is now being served in the foyer; soon the door to the banquet hall will open for all who want to enter and enjoy the feast. That will happen when the King appears the second time.

The Marriage Supper

At that time when Jesus returns, all who have said yes to him will join in a great wedding celebration. That is the astonishing description of the relationship between Jesus Christ and the church. He is the bridegroom. The church is his bride.

The appetizer is already being served. Yet the full and bounteous banquet awaits the day when Jesus will return. On that day, peoples from every tribe and nation and language will gather with joy and praise at the wedding banquet with Jesus in heaven.

The wedding invitations have been sent out. Welcome! To all who want to come, welcome!

John writes in the concluding pages of the Bible,

> Then I heard what sounded like a great multitude, like the roar of rushing waters and like loud peals of thunder, shouting:
>> Hallelujah!
>> For our Lord God Almighty reigns.
>> Let us rejoice and be glad
>> and give him glory!
>> For the wedding of the Lamb has come,
>> and his bride has made herself ready.
>
> Fine linen, bright and clean, was given her to wear. (Rev. 19:6-8) [Fine linen stands for the righteous acts of the saints.]

• • •

The story of a father and his two sons is a revelation of God as revealed in Jesus Christ.

Everyone was astonished to see the father abandoning his dignity as he ran through the village to welcome and embrace his rebellious younger son. At the feast that followed, the older son staged a boycott. We are like those sons, who embarrass and grieve their father, although the father welcomes both sons to his banquet.

If God is like that father, then all peoples in all cultures and all religions should be invited to the life-giving banquet.

Not everything in our cultures or personal practices are worthy of the banquet. The invitation to the banquet is also an invitation to personal and cultural transformation; it is an invitation to repentance. We need the clean and handsome robes provided by the Father who hosts the banquet.

One day the whole earth will be astonished and speechless, for Jesus will come again. That day will be the final and great divide of all history. All are invited to the banquet. Some have chosen to remain outside, while others accept the invitation with thankfulness and great joy.

The banquet Jesus is preparing is like a joyous marriage feast. The church is the bride. Jesus is the bridegroom. A feast is at hand; welcome.

14

SO WHAT?

In his first miracle Jesus surprised a wedding party when he turned water to wine in Cana near his hometown of Nazareth (Chapter 7). He also preached his first sermon in Nazareth in the neighborhood where he had grown up. In that sermon in the synagogue during Saturday morning worship, Jesus announced the beginning of his public ministry. The townsfolk who knew him well were present that day.

First he read his sermon text from the Prophet Isaiah:

> The Spirit of the Lord is on me,
>> because he has anointed me
>> to preach good news to the poor.
> He has sent me to proclaim freedom
>> for the prisoners
>> and recovery of sight for the blind,
> to release the oppressed,
>> to proclaim the year of the Lord's favor.
> (Luke 4:18-19)

Then he preached. The sermon was one sentence. "Today this Scripture is fulfilled in your hearing" (Luke 4:21).

The whole synagogue was astir with delight and expectation. They questioned and listened to Jesus.

Jesus reminded them of several past occasions when the people of Israel turned away from God and missed out on God's salvation, while Gentiles turned to God and received salvation.

The mood in the synagogue changed from happy expectation to dismay and tension. The Gentiles were not friends of the people in Nazareth; the Roman Gentiles were their oppressors. They did not want Gentiles to become part of their community of godly faith.

However, Jesus continued to explain forthrightly that Gentiles would be included in the salvation that he was proclaiming. Jesus warned them that being the genealogical descendants of Abraham and Sarah was not a guarantee that they would receive salvation.

As Jesus spoke about the vastness of God's plan for the salvation of the nations, the atmosphere in that Saturday worship transformed dramatically from one of gracious piety to furious anger and seething hate.

In anger, the congregation seized Jesus and rushed him to a brow of a nearby hill hoping to throw him off a cliff to his death. He walked through the crowd, however, and went on his way.

One of the surprises of the Christian Way is that those one might expect to receive the Lord's favor turn away, and those one might expect to be far away from the Lord, draw near. The Lord's favor is for all who will come.

The presence of the kingdom of God is the good news of the Lord's favor. His favor is for all people.

So What?

As Jesus walked the paths of Palestine, he occasionally startled a person by inviting, "Follow me!"

He called people to follow him most unexpectedly. For example: Matthew sitting at his tax collecting table; Peter and John fishing with their dad; Zacchaeus hiding in a huge tree; Mary who was filled with seven demons; other women likewise became followers of Jesus.

Today also, Jesus, through his Sprit, through the church, through the Scriptures, through our circumstances, and in many other ways, calls, "Follow me!" To follow Jesus is a gift of astounding grace, because of who Jesus is.

Jesus surprises us with this invitation,

> Come to me, all you who are weary and burdened, and I will give you rest. Take my yoke on you and learn from me, for I am gentle and humble in heart, and you will find rest for your souls. For my yoke is easy and my burden is light. (Matt. 11:28-30)

Jesus invites, "Follow me!"

To trust Jesus Christ is to receive the Lord's favor. To follow Jesus is to discover the joyful surprises of the Christian Way.

STUDY GUIDE
SURPRISES OF
THE CHRISTIAN WAY

Chapter 1: The God Riddle

Background Scripture: Genesis 3:8-10; Exodus 3:1-15.

1. Give reasons why many people consider God to be a problem.

2. Consider the ten approaches to the God riddle. Comment on any that are especially attractive. Reflect on reasons for the attraction.

3. God himself addresses the God riddle by meeting us. Consider the significance of God meeting Adam and Eve in Genesis 3:8-10 and God meeting Moses in Exodus 3:1-15. Has God met you or any of your friends?

4. Read Genesis 1. In what ways is God as described in these paragraphs different than the understandings of God among your acquaintances?

Chapter 2: The Good Earth

Background Scripture: Genesis 1

1. The earth and universe provide overwhelming evidence that there is a Creator. Account for the reasons that many people choose not to believe in God (Rom. 1:18-23).

2. Note the four alternatives to the belief that the good earth is God's creation. Why are they attractive?

3. Consider the five biblical foundations for the scientific revolution (Gen. 1). Perhaps you would like to test these principles with a scientist and see if she agrees that these principles are necessary in order for science to thrive.

4. Are you aware of areas of possible conflict between science and biblical faith? If so, what are reasons for that conflict?

5. The Anabaptists preached frequently from Psalms 24:1. In what ways does the church in your community reveal the truth of this text?

Chapter 3: The Wise Ones

Background Scripture: Genesis 1:26-31; 2:7, 15-25.

1. Do you agree with the statement that debates about when the earth was formed detract from the core differences between evolutionary theory and biblical faith? Give reasons for your agreement or disagreement.

2. Reflect on the three core differences between biblical faith and evolutionary theory that are described in this chapter. Do you think of other differences? What are they (Gen. 1, Phil. 2:3-11)?

3. In what ways does the biblical teaching that both man and woman are equally created in God's image and that the essence of marriage as one flesh union lay the foundations for joyful marriage (Gen. 1:27; 2:21-25)?

4. Consider reasons why whole social systems in our century have embraced the cruelty of evolutionary theory.

5. Have you experienced or observed the power of love for the other? Give examples.

Chapter 4: The Enemy Invades

Background Scripture: Genesis 3:1-4:9; Revelation 22:1-3.

1. Account for the reality of sinfulness (Gen. 3:1-11).

2. Reflect on the meaning of the tree of knowledge of good and evil (Gen. 2:16, 17; 3:1-7). What is the true source for

knowing good and evil? Account for the confusion concerning right and wrong that we experience when we choose to ignore God.

3. List the ten consequences of turning away from God mentioned in Genesis 3:7-4:9. In what ways do you observe in your community these consequences of declaring independence from God?

4. Consider ways we might use religion as a camouflage of our true selves (Gen. 3:7; Matt. 6:5-7).

Chapter 5: The Interception

Background Scripture:
Genesis 3:15; Isaiah 9:6-7; Matthew 1:21- 22.

1. In what ways have you experienced this to be true: God has not abandoned us.

2. Describe times when you have felt that God has abandoned you.

2. Reflect on the meaning of hope. Discuss this statement: Biblical faith gives hope (Matt. 1:21-22).

3. What does redemption mean? What is the difference between a rescue and redemption (Luke 19:1-10)?

Chapter 6: A People of Hope

Background Scripture: Genesis 12.

1. What is the meaning of a "root experience"? Have you ever encountered such an experience personally? If so, reflect on the significance of that experience for your own life.

2. List the five Old Testament biblical root events described in this chapter.

3. Select one of the five events above and consider the significance of that event for us today.

4. What does it mean to be a blessing to the nations (Gen. 12:3)? Do you consider the church today to be a blessing to the nations? Give reasons for your response.

Chapter 7: Immanuel

Background Scripture: Luke 1:26-2:20

1. Reflect on why outsiders (shepherds and wise men from the east) were the first to celebrate the birth of Jesus (Luke 2:8-20; Matt. 2:1-12). Does this happen today? Give reasons.

2. Religious people without compassion angered Jesus (Mark 3:1- 6). Consider modern examples.

3. Discuss this statement: The Sermon on the Mount is good news (Matt. 5-7).

4. Give reasons for the tremendous controversy Jesus experienced when he forgave sins (Mark 2:1-12).

5. Jesus claimed to be the Son of God (Mark 14:61-62). What are the alternatives? Who do you believe that Jesus is? Explain your choice.

Chapter 8: The Colt Rider

Background Scripture: Luke 19:28-48.

1. What did it mean for Jesus to ride a colt into Jerusalem (Luke 19:28-44; Zech. 9:9,10)?

2. Give reasons why the religious authorities were so disturbed (Zech. 9:9,10).

3. Explain the reasons Jesus refused the offer to become king after he fed the five thousand (John 6:1-15).

4. Reflect on the reasons the people of Jericho were so offended when Jesus had dinner in the home of Zacchaeus (Luke 19:1-10).

5. What kind of king is Jesus? What do you make of him? Should *you* take him seriously? Give reasons for your answer (John 18:36,37).

Chapter 9: The Lamb and the Scroll

Background Scripture: Revelation 5

1. Consider the consequences of persons, systems, or religions claiming the authority to direct history (Rev. 5:1-4).

2. What is the significance of Jesus as Lion of Judah, Root of David, and slain Lamb? Give reasons why the slain Lamb metaphor is especially significant (Rev. 5:5-7).

3. Comment on this statement: Forgiveness is exceedingly costly. In what ways does the crucifixion of Jesus demonstrate how costly forgiveness is for God (Matt. 26:27,28)?

4. If God is sovereign, why doesn't he just forgive? Reflect on why we're forgiven only in Jesus crucified (1 Pet. 2:24).

5. The church is called to forgive as Jesus forgave. Several Christians in Mostar offered themselves in sacrificial service, standing between the hostile forces and offering the gift of forgiveness and reconciliation in Christ. Consider other examples of the church becoming a sacrificial and reconciling people.

6. Jesus' sacrifice reconciles us with each other and God (Col. 1:21,22). What is our responsibility in reconciliation?

Chapter 10: The Power of God
Background Scripture: Matthew 28

1. Does your society assume that violence is needed to maintain law and order? (Note that in some societies police are unarmed.) How do you feel about the assumptions about violence in your society? What would Jesus do (Matt. 5:38-48)?

2. Comment on this statement: The cross is the most significant difference of the Christian faith when compared to other religions and ideologies (1 Cor. 1:22-25).

3. The cross is the power of God for those who are being saved. What does that mean (1 Cor. 1:18)?

4. Six dimensions of the mystery of Jesus crucified and risen are discussed in this chapter. Comment on each one.

Chapter 11: The Coach and the Team
Background Scripture: Acts 1:1-11; 2:1-47.

1. Explain why Jesus referred to the Holy Spirit as a counselor or advocate (John 14:16, 26; 15:26; 16:7-15).

2. Why did Jesus not give his disciples any detailed plan or organization for implementing his kingdom (Acts 1:4-8)?

3. Describe the birthday of the church. Consider the significance of that birthday happening during the Jewish Feast of Harvest (Acts 2:1-41).

4. Comment on this statement: The most significant development of the twentieth century is the global spread of the church.

5. How is it possible for the church to celebrate both diversity and unity (Acts 15:1-35)?

6. What is joy? Account for the joy when people gather together in Jesus' name (Matt. 18:20; John 15:9-12).

7. Give examples of churches expressing care for people. Are you aware of failures of the church to express care?

Chapter 12: The Message
Background Scripture: Matthew 28:16-20, Acts 1:6-8.

1. Give reasons for the importance of Scripture in the life and mission of the church (Luke 1:1-4; John 20:30-31).

2. Why are trustworthy Gospel accounts of the life and teachings of Jesus important for the church in its mission?

3. Are you surprised that in the second century there was a great debate about the Old Testament? Account for the debate about whether the Old Testament should be included in the Christian Bible. Comment on the significance of the Old Testament for Christians.

4. What does a Christ-centered biblical hermeneutic mean?

Chapter 13: The Banquet
Background Scripture: Luke 15:11-32

1. What have you learned about God as our Father through the story of a father and his two sons (Luke 15:11-32)?

2. In what ways might you identify with the younger son? The older son?

3. What are some of the objections people have against Christian missions? What can the church learn from those objections? Why did Jesus commission the church to take the gospel to all peoples?

4. Consider this statement: The truth that God is love is more powerful than armies (1 Cor. 1:22-25).

5. Reflect on reasons people sometimes choose to be absent from the banquet Jesus is hosting.

6. How does the promise of Jesus that he will return again give Christians hope (Matt. 26:64)?

7. Comment on this statement: Jesus is the great divide of human history (Matt. 25:31-46).

NOTES

Chapter 1

1. Carla Power, "Lost in Silent Prayer," *Newsweek* (July 12, 1999), 50.

2. *Ibid.*, 51.

3. Sigmund Freud, *The Future of an Illusion*, trans. W. D. Robson-Scott and revised and ed. James Strachey (London: The Brown Knight & Truscott Group, 1973).

4. John Miller, "The Message of the Bible," *The Mennonite* (July, 20, 1999), 6, 7. (In John's essay he writes of four dramas, viewing the New Testament as one drama.)

5. W. F. Albright, *From the Stone Age to Christianity* (New York: Doubleday, 1957), 249, 272.

6. Emil Fackenheim, *The Presence of God in History: Jewish Affirmations and Philosophical Reflections* (New York: New York University Press, 1970), 8-14.

Chapter 2

1. Sharon Begley, "When Galaxies Collide," *Newsweek* (November 3, 1997), 36.

2. Nicholas Wade, "A Worm Yields the First Full DNA Multi-celled Mapping," (New York Times Service), *International Herald Tribune* (December 12-13, 1998), 2.

3. Ibid.

4. Paul Davies, *The Mind of God, The Scientific Basis for a Rational World* (New York: Simon and Schuster, 1992), 198-200.

5. Karen Long, "New Discoveries Energize Science/Religion Debate," *Mennonite Weekly Review* (May 6, 1999), 3.

6. Arend Theodoor van Leeuwen, *Christianity in World History*, trans. H. H. Hoskins (New York: Charles H. Scribners Sons, 1964), 158-165.

7. Walter Wink, *Unmasking the Powers* (Philadelphia: Fortress, 1986), 135.

8. *Carey's Obligation and India's Renaissance*, ed. J. T. K. Daniel and R. E. Hedlund (Serampore: Council of Serampore College, 1993), 259-298.

Chapter 3

1. Tim Stafford, "The Making of a Revolution," *Christianity Today* (Carol Stream: Christianity Today, Inc., December 8, 1997), 16-22.

Michael Denton, *Evolution: A Theory in Crisis* (Bethesda, Md.: Adler and Adler, 1986).

2. Walter Trobisch, *I Married You* (San Francisco: HarperSanFrancisco, 1989), 21-24.

Chapter 4

1. *Christian Reflections*, "Christianity and Culture," ed. Walter Hooper (Grand Rapids, Mich.: Wm. B. Eerdmans Publishing Co., 1967), 33

2. M. Scott Peck, *People of the Lie, The Hope for Healing Human Evil* (New York: Simon and Schuster, 1983), 129.

3. Paul Tournier, *The Meaning of Persons* (New York: Harper & Row, 1957), 179-197.

4. Dietrich Bonhoeffer, *Letters and Papers from Prison*, ed. Eberhard Bethge (London: SCM Press Ltd., 1973), 278-282.

5. Eloise Maneses, *Leadership and Family Structures* (Black Rock, Pa.: Lectures, EMM Discernment and Enrichment Retreat, July, 1997).

6. Sigmund Freud, *Totem and Taboo*, trans. A. A. Brill (New York: Vintage Books, 1946).

Chapter 5

1. Malcolm J. McVeigh, *God in Africa* (Hartford, Conn.: Claude Stark, 1974), 48,49.

2. John S. Mbiti, *Concepts of God in Africa* (London: SPCK, 1971), 177.

3. Jurgen Moltmann, *Theology of Hope, On the Ground and*

Implications of a Christian Eschatology (New York: Harper & Row, 1975).

4. C.K. Leaman, *Biblical Theology: Old Testament*, Vol. I (Scottdale: Herald Press, @date?), 65.

5. B. F. Skinner, *Beyond Freedom and Dignity* (New York: Knopf, 1971).

Chapter 6

1. W. F. Albright, 249, 272.

2. Fackenheim, 8-14.

3. Walter Wink, *Engaging the Powers* (Minneapolis: Fortress Press, 1912), 13-17

4. Joseph C. Shenk, *David, Search for Legitimacy*, Thesis, Master of Arts in Religion (Harrisonburg: Eastern Mennonite University, 1996).

5. Millard C. Lind, *Yahweh is a Warrior* (Scottdale, Pa.: Herald Press, 1980).

Chapter 7

1. C. S. Lewis, *Surprised by Joy: the Shape of My Early Life* (New York: Harcourt, 1956).

2. Tony Campolo, *The Kingdom of God is a Party* (Dallas: Word, 1992).

3. Philip Yancey, *The Jesus I Never Knew* (Grand Rapids: Zondervan, 1995), 165-182.

4. Jurgen Moltmann, *The Way of Jesus Christ* (San Francisco: Harper-San Francisco, 1990) 99.

5. C. S. Lewis, *Mere Christianity* (New York: The Macmillan Company, 1960), 56.

Chapter 8

1. Kevin D. Miller, "The War of the Scrolls," *Christianity Today* (October 6, 1997), 40-45.

2. Donald Kraybill, *The Upside Down Kingdom* (Scottdale, Pa.: Herald Press, 1978), 66-68, 86, 87.

3. Kenneth E. Bailey, Scripture meditation shared at a worship event at a meeting of Evangelicals for Middle East Understanding, North West College, Chicago, October, 1996.

Chapter 9

1. *Menno Simons, A Reappraisal, Essays in honor of Irvin B. Horst*

on the 450th anniversary of the Fundamentboek, ed. Gerald R. Brunk (Harrisonburg, Va.: Eastern Mennonite University, 1992), 111.

2. Oswald Chambers, *My Utmost for His Highest* (Westwood: Barbour and Company, 1963), 97

3. Rene Girard, *Violence and the Sacred*, trans. Patrick Gregory (Baltimore: Johns Hopkins University Press, 1981), 1-67, 250-273.

4. Miroslav Volf, *Exclusion and Embrace* (Nashville: Abingdon Press, 1996), 292-295.

5. Gerard Kelly and Lowell Sheppard, *Miracle in Mostar* (Oxford: Lion, 1995).

Chapter 10

1. Wink, 15.

2. *Ibid.*, 17.

3. Hans Kung, *On Being a Christian*, trans. Edward Quinn (New York: Simon and Schuster, 1978), 410.

4. Brunk, 10.

Chapter 11

1. William G. Young, *Handbook of Source Materials for Students of Church History, Up to A.D. 650* (Madras: The Christian Literature Society, 1969), 19

2. John P. Kealy and David W. Shenk, *The Early Church and Africa* (Nairobi: Oxford University Press, 1975), 175-187.

3. David Barrett, *World Class Cities and World Evangelization* (Birmingham: New Hope, 1986), 54.

4. Marshall V. King, "1,000,000 Anabaptists," *Mennonite Weekly Review* (Newton: Herald Publishing, January 1, 1998), 1.

5. *Ibid.*

6. W. B. Anderson, *The Church in East Africa, 1840-1974* (Dodoma: Central Tanzania Press, 1977), 97-98.6

Chapter 12

1. Young, Section 63.

2. Kealy and Shenk, 293, 294.

3. *The New International Study Bible*, ed. Kenneth Baker (Grand Rapids: Zondervan, 1985), 1437, 1591. John A. T. Robinson, *Redating the New Testament* (London: SCM, 1975), 13-32.

4. Yancey, 261-263.

5. M. Scott Peck, *Further Along the Road Less Traveled* (New York: Simon and Schuster, 1993), 160.

6. Nevin D. Miller, "The War of the Scrolls," *Christianity Today* (Carol Stream, Ill.: Christianity Today, Inc., October 6, 1997), 38-45.

7. Sean Kealy, *Our Changing Bible* (Nairobi: Kenyatta University College, N.D.), 87.

8. Robert L. Lindsey, *A Hebrew Translation of the Gospel of Mark, Greek-Hebrew Diglot* with foreword by David Flusser (Jerusalem: Dugith Publishers, 1973) and *The Jesus Sources: Understanding the Gospels* (Tulsa: Hakesher, 1990).

Chapter 13

1. Kenneth E. Bailey, *The Cross and the Prodigal* (St. Lewis: Concordia, 1973) and Henri J. M. Nouwen, *The Return of the Prodigal Son* (New York: Doubleday, 1992).

2. Nouwen, 93-102.

SELECT BIBLIOGRAPHY
FOR FURTHER READING

Anderson, Sir Norman. *Jesus Christ: the Witness of History*. Downers Grove: InterVarsity Press, 1985.

Augsburger, Myron S. *The Christ-Shaped Conscience*. Wheaton: Victor Books, 1990.

Bailey, Kenneth E. *The Cross and the Prodigal*. St. Louis: Concordia. 1973.

Bainton, Roland H. *Behold the Christ*. New York: Harper & Row, 1974.

Barclay, William. *Jesus As They Saw Him*. Grand Rapids, Mich.: Wm. B. Eerdmans Publishing Co, 1962.

Berkhof, Hendrik. *Christ and the Powers*. Scottdale, Pa.: Herald Press, 1977.

Bonhoeffer, Dietrich. *Christ the Center*. San Francisco: Harper & Rowe, 1978.

———. *The Cost of Discipleship*. New York: Macmillan, 1961.

Bosch, David J. *A Spirituality of the Road*. Scottdale, Pa.: Herald Press, 1979.

Bright, John. *The Kingdom of God: The Biblical Concept and Its Meaning for the Church*. Nashville: Abingdon Press, 1983.

Brunk, Gerald R., ed. *Menno Simons. A Reappraisal. Essays in honor of Irvin B. Horst on the 450th anniversary of the Fundamentboek.* Harrisonburg, Va.: Eastern Mennonite University, 1992.

Campolo, Tony. *The Kingdom of God is a Party.* Dallas: Word, 1992.

Carter, Stephen L. *The Culture of Disbelief.* New York: HarperCollins, 1993.

Clendenin, Daniel B.. *Christianity Encouters World Religions. Many Gods Many Lords.* Grand Rapids: Baker, 1995.

Conn, Harvie M. *Eternal Word and Changing Worlds: Theology. Anthropology. and Mission in Trialogue.* Grand Rapids: Zondervan, 1984.

Covell, Ralph R. *Pluralism: Challenge to World Religions.* Maryknoll, N.Y.: Orbis, 1985.

Cragg, Kenneth. *To Meet and To Greet: Faith with Faith.* Westminster: Epworth Press, 1992.

Dodd, C. H. *The Founder of Christianity.* London: The Macmillan Company, 1970.

Dyck, Cornelius J. *Spiritual Life in Anabaptism.* Scottdale, Pa.: Herald Press, 1995.

Ellul, Jacques. *The Subversion of Chrisianity.* Trans. Geoffrey W. Bromiley. Grand Rapids: Wm. B. Eerdmans Publishing Co., 1986.

Foster, Richard J. *Money, Sex, and Power.* San Francisco: Harper & Row, 1985.

———. *Prayer.* San Franciscio: Harper, 1992.

Hughes, Dewi Arwel. *Has God Many Names? An Introduction to Religious Studies.* Leicester: Apollos, 1996.

Jacobs, Donald R. *Pilgrimage in Mission.* Scottdale, Pa.: Herald Press, 1983.

Kateregga, Badru D. and David W. Shenk. *A Muslim and a Christian in Dialogue*. Scottdale, Pa.: Herald Press, 1997.

Kreider, Alan. *Journey Towards Holiness*. Scottdale, Pa.: Herald Press, 1987.

Kraus, Norman C. *The Authentic Witness: Credibility and Authority*. Scottdale, Pa.: Herald Press, 1990.

Kung, Hans. *On Being a Christian*. Trans. Edward Quinn. New York: Simon and Schuster, 1978.

Ladd, George Eldon. *The Gospel of the Kingdom*. Grand Rapids: Wm. B. Eerdmans Publishing Co., 1981.

Lehman, Chester K. *The Holy Spirit and the Holy Life*. Scottdale, Pa.: Herald Press, 1959.

Lewis, C. S. *Mere Christianity* New York: The Macmillan Company, 1960.

———. *Miracles*. London: Collins, 1947.

———. *Surprised by Joy: the Shape of My Early Life*. New York: Harcourt, 1956.

Macquarrie, John. *The Humility of God*. Philadelphia: The Westminster Press, 1978.

———. *Jesus in Modern Thought*. Philadelphia: Trinity Press, 1990.

Moltmann, Jurgen. *The Crucified God*. New York: Harper & Row, 1974.

———. *Theology of Hope*. San Francisco: Harper & Row, 1975.

Mosher, Steve. *God's Power, Jesus' Faith and World Mission. A Study in Romans*. Scottdale, Pa.: Herald Press, 1996.

Muggeridge, Malcolm. *Jesus: the Man Who Lives*. New York: Harper & Row, 1975.

Neill, Stephen. *Christian Faith and Other Faiths*. London: Oxford University Press, 1970.

Newbigin, Lesslie. *Foolishness to the Greeks: The Gospel and Western Culture.* Grand Rapids: Wm. B. Eerdmans Publishing Co., 1986.

———. *The Gospel in a Pluralist Society.* Grand Rapids: Wm. B. Eerdmans Publishing Co., 1989.

———. *Honest Religion for Secular Man.* London: SCM, 1966.

———. *Mission in Christ's Way.* New York: Friendship Press, 1987.

———. *Truth to Tell. The Gospel as Public Truth.* Grand Rapids: Wm. B. Eerdmans Publishing Co., 1991.

Nouwen, Henri J. M. *The Return of the Prodigal Son.* New York: Doubleday, 1992.

Peck, M. Scott. *People of the Lie. The Hope for Healing Human Evil.* New York: Simon and Schuster, 1983.

Phillips, J. B. *Good News.* London: Geofrey Bles, 1964.

———. *New Testament Christianity.* London: Hodder and Stoughton, 1958.

———. *The Ring of Truth.* Wheaton: Harold Shaw Publishers, 1977.

———. *Your God is Too Small.* New York: Macmillan, 1960.

Pinnock, Clark H. *A Wideness in God's Mercy. The Finality of Jesus Christ in a World of Religions.* Grand Rapids: Zondervan, 1992.

Pippert, Rebecca Manley. *Out of the Saltshaker and into the World.* Downers Grove, Ill.: InterVarsity Press, 1979.

Richardson, Don. *Eternity in Their Hearts.* Ventura: Regal, 1984.

Sanneh, Lamin. *Translating the Message.* Maryknoll: Orbis, 1989.

Schaeffer, Francis. *The God Who is There.* London: Hodder and Stoughton, 1973.

————. *The Mark of a Christian.* London: InterVarsity Press, 1971.

Scott, Waldron. *Bring Forth Justice: A Contemporary Perspective on Mission.* Grand Rapids: Wm. B. Eerdmans Publishing Co., 1980.

Shenk, Calvin E. *Who Do You Say That I Am? Christians Encounter Other Religions.* Scottdale, Pa.: Herald Press, 1997.

Shenk, David W. and Ervin R. Stutzman. *Creating Communities of the Kingdom.* Scottdale, Pa.: Herald Press, 1988.

————. *Global Gods. Exploring the Role of Religions in Modern Societies.* Scottdale, Pa.: Herald Press, 1995.

————. *God's Call to Mission.* Scottdale, Pa.: Herald Press, 1994.

————. *Justice, Reconciliation, and Peace in Africa.* Nairobi: Uzima, 1997.

Sider, Ronald J. *Rich Christians in an Age of Hunger.* Downers Grove: InterVarsity Press, 1982.

Stutzman, Linford. *With Jesus in the World: Mission in Modern, Affluent Societies.* Scottdale, Pa.: Herald Press, 1990.

Trueblood, Elton. *The Company of the Committed.* New York: Harper & Row, 1961.

————. *The Incendiary Fellowship.* New York: Harper & Row. n.d.

————. *The New Man for our Time.* New York: Harper & Row, 1970.

————. *The Validity of the Christian Mission.* New York: Harper & Row, 1972.

Wagner, C. Peter. *Prayer Shield.* Ventura: Regal, 1992.

Wallis, Jim. *The Call to Conversion.* San Francisco: Harper & Row, 1981.

Wenger, J. C. *God's Word Written.* Scottdale, Pa.: Herald Press, 1968.

Wink, Walter. *Engaging the Powers.* Minneapolis: Fortress, 1992.

————. *Unmasking the Powers: The Invisible Forces that Determine Human Existence.* Philadelphia: Fortress Press, 1986.

Yancey, Philip. *Disappointed with God.* Grand Rapids: Zondervon, 1988.

————. *The Jesus I Never Knew.* Grand Rapids: Zondervan, 1995.

Yoder, John Howard. *The Original Revolution.* Scottdale, Pa.: Herald Press, 1972.

————. *The Politics of Jesus.* Grand Rapids: Wm. B. Eerdmans Publishing Co., 1972.

THE AUTHOR

David W. Shenk is academic dean and professor of theology at Lithuania Christian College, Klaipeda, Lithuania. He served for nearly two decades as director of U.S. missions and then overseas ministries for Eastern Mennonite Missions, Salunga, Pennsylvania. He is author of many articles and books on religion and mission, including the award-winning *Global Gods* (Herald Press, 1995) and *Christians and Muslims in Dialogue* (with Badru Katerrega, Herald Press, 1997). Recently he co-edited (with Linford Stutzman) *Practicing Truth: Christian Witness in Our Pluralistic Word* (Herald Press, 1999).